Is Your Mind really Yours?

Break Free from the Shackles of a Programmed Life

Ajay Sachdeva

PAPER MISSILE

NIYOGI BOOKS

Published by
NIYOGI BOOKS
Block D, Building No. 77,
Okhla Industrial Area, Phase-I,
New Delhi-110 020, INDIA
Tel: 91-11-26816301, 26818960
Email: niyogibooks@gmail.com
Website: www.niyogibooksindia.com

Editor: Saachi Khurana
Design: Nabanita Das

ISBN: 978-93-86906-04-5
Publication: 2017

Printed at: Niyogi Offset Pvt. Ltd., New Delhi, India

Dedicated to my loving father, Gulshan Rai Sachdeva—the epitome of selflessness and unremitting love. One who gave of himself to others freely and unconditionally. Memories of the wonderful moments we spent together are fondly cherished. You are my inspiration for this book, Dad.

Acclaim for *Is Your Mind Really Yours?*

Ajay Sachdeva…has done a great job in demystifying the complex mind and presenting it beautifully in the context of our day-to-day living.

Ashok Wahi
Former CEO, Lemuir Group
Life coach and healer

The author is lucid, readable and truthful.

S.K. Bhatia
Former executive director, General Electric Corporation of India
Award-winning writer

An extremely thought-provoking text that compels the reader to understand his own self and beliefs that he thinks are of his own making.

Rajiv Walia
Managing editor, Asia News Agency

A must-read for all who strive to discover the 'divine intelligence' residing in our hearts so as to cleanse what the author calls our 'conditioned' mind.

Gautam Bakhshi
Business consultant

The concept of trusting our conviction instead of seeking continuous validation from others about being on the right path has been my key takeaway from this book.

Hitesh Chandel
Chief mentor of Defined Values Consultants
Author of *Code of Citizen's Conduct*

His book is a must-read for those in search of becoming better human beings.

Percy Batlivala
Former Chairman and Founder
Indian Institute of Retail Training

Contents

Foreword

The author has been bestowed with much to be grateful for, though a set of untoward circumstances made him question life's fairness. It was during some turbulent phases that the seeds of his spiritual quest were sown. Thus, his journey began to find answers to several perplexing questions that, at some time or the other, plague all of us.

Ajay made several attempts to understand the workings of life through various spiritual practices. While there was much knowledge acquired, wisdom was still elusive. It took him quite some time to realise that wisdom can never come from trying to figure out life from the 'outside'. Nor can any learnings that are indoctrinated from the external world become the truth of one's life if they don't resonate with one's inner self. Often, these end up conditioning oneself with 'borrowed' knowledge. It dawned upon the author that, instead of trying to figure out life from an 'external' approach, one would need to figure out life through a method that focused on the 'inner' self.

Life in many ways is not always kind to us—we face ups and downs along the way—and Ajay provides a matchless method of getting through hard times.The book delves into many of the root causes of unhappiness, strife and discontentment. It is divided into seven chapters, each dealing with different, major aspects of life.

This book is intended to stimulate the readers to revisit their life's journey with as much objectivity as possible.There is, of course, no one-size-fits-all solution to people's problems. This book, however, attempts to incorporate a broad range of issues that typically afflict everyone.The contents of the book fully justify the title, *Is Your Mind Really* Yours? It places a unique emphasis on *reclaiming* one's mind, that is, taking it back from the influence and conditioning of external, possibly erroneous ideas. Quotes from several well-known personalities show how the author has invested much time and effort into his highly readable book. A case is presented to the readers for them to consider rising above the 'wrongs' and 'rights' of the perspectives that may have been imposed on them. The interactive nature of the book vis-à-vis the fundamental questions raised encourages readers to actively think about their lives.

Is Your Mind Really Yours? is a culmination of learnings from the author's myriad experiences, the observations of nature and its phenomena, and the interactions with people from many walks of life, all of which played their part in helping him deduce his inner truth.

I thank Ajay for giving me the honour of writing the foreword for his book.

D.R. Kaarthikeyan

Former director, Central Bureau of Investigation

Advisor for Law, Human Rights and Corporate Affairs

Introduction

Life in many ways has been very kind to me, and I have a sense of deep gratitude for all that I have been blessed with. However, like many of us, I too have had my share of extremely low moments, triggered by certain events that shook me. It is largely in such moments that one's spiritual quest as a seeker begins, in terms of finding answers to a set of perplexing questions that plague us. It is common to turn to various spiritual practices in the hope that there will be handy solutions given to us on a platter.

While I respected the essence of the philosophies that many spiritual practices had to offer, I realised that no philosophy would work for me if it did not strike a chord of an 'inner' resonance. After all, blindly following any practice would only be an imposition, not something that truly connected with my heart. Thus began my journey, spanning years of introspection, of learning from a multitude of experiences, reading several books on spirituality while being an observer of nature and its phenomena. In the process, I realised that for one's inner truth to reveal itself, one needed to stop trying to figure out the external world. What one needed to do was just figure oneself out.

This book, a culmination of all my efforts in understanding the self, is intended to stimulate the readers to dispassionately revisit their life's journey so far. It invites them to carry out an honest exploration of *who they really are* and the relationship they have with themselves. The underlying premise is that it is only in the knowing of one's *true* self that one can liberate oneself from the shackles of an illusory and caged existence, which becomes the cause of one's misery. Life is essentially centred around the relationship one has with one's self (with one's thoughts, feelings and emotions), which in turn determines the relationship with one's external world, comprising spouses, families, friends, workplace, and so on.

The book makes no pretensions about injecting its readers with doses of any new dogmas, sermons, laws or prescriptions about how they need to lead their lives. Instead it provokes them to re-examine and question various belief systems they may have closely guarded and held. Any belief system or advice invariably emanates from the aggregate of external sources, is therefore 'borrowed' and hence can only end up *conditioning* the minds of individuals. As a result, any indoctrination usually becomes stifling, binding and limiting and acts as the prime barrier in letting individuals live a life that is truly theirs. It also denies them the space to strive for all that they wish for in the deepest recesses of their hearts.

As a consequence, some fundamental questions have been raised in the book to provide food for thought. For instance: Are we, in our conditioned state, living a life that is akin to a computer hardware that has been programmed to operate only in a certain way? Or for that matter like a caged bird that is bereft of the freedom to fly and to live according to its true nature? Have we handed over the remote control of our lives to others, whom we allow to determine our state of mind, in fact our thoughts, behaviours and even key decisions? Are we honestly living authentic lives, being true to ourselves?

The answers to such questions must only come from our readers. While they reflect on their own answers, a case is presented for them to consider rising above all the 'wrongs' and 'rights' of the perspectives that may have been *imposed* on them, as also the multitude of belief systems they would have accepted as their life's reality.

The aspect of being true to oneself and operating from the 'free spirit' as an alternative to operating from the ego dimension and the programmed mind, thereby experiencing **freedom, growth and contentment**, forms the crux and cornerstone of this book.

The book comprises of seven chapters:

Chapter one is about rediscovering one's true self, going beyond the tags, labels and embellishments we attach ourselves to, and introspecting on who we truly are. The premise is that only the 'knowing' and experiencing of our true selves can enable us to come out of our trapped and 'caged' existence. It also makes a submission that much of the turmoil, chaos and suffering that humankind experiences is a consequence of not being in awareness of *who we truly are.*

Chapter two talks about the vital significance of the relationship we have with ourselves, which is invariably ignored, and how this governs and impacts our relationship with our world.

Chapter three focuses on aspects related to the relationship we have with our circumstances, with a submission that, while these may *influence* our life condition, they don't necessarily have to *determine* it. It goes on to present a premise that much of our suffering is actually 'manufactured' in the mind rather than being a consequence of events happening outside of us.

Chapter four dwells on the many myths built around love and on how, in a marriage, programmed minds can distort and adversely affect our relationships. It stimulates thinking on whether marriage, love and freedom can harmoniously coexist and, if so, on what it would take to make it happen.

Chapter five examines our relationships with family (parents, children, in-laws, and so on), friends and society, stressing the fact that when we operate from a programmed mind, we experience turbulence and discord. It is only through a 'reprogramming' that drops conditioned mindsets that harmonious relationships can be experienced.

Chapter six discusses our relationships with our jobs and businesses, and the increasing challenges we face in a highly uncertain and chaotic environment. It makes a case for integrating the essence of spirituality into our work cultures. Unleashing one's creativity and bringing in innovation at the workplace is possible only once we detach ourselves from the programmed minds that invariably limit us.

Finally, chapter seven summarises the essence of a liberating journey, which can be experienced when we make choices out of awareness and in alignment with our true self.

In sum, whilst this book does not aim to present any new philosophy to its readers, it certainly attempts to prompt the readers into examining life from another perspective—*the setting free of all ideas, opinions, and stereotypes*—all that the mind has gotten entangled with and which never belonged to individuals in the first place. It is in this letting go and establishing the connection with the true self that they can begin to feel the liberation that was always within them but got caged in the mental trap.

You will find that the book is peppered with boxed quotes from eminent writers, spiritualists and philosophers. This is because it was felt that the quotes, whilst striking a deep chord of inner resonance, were relevant to the context and served to add substance to the subject matter.

It is my fervent hope that as readers go through the contents of the book, they will find themselves realising the vast potential of their real self and awaken to their true nature as they consciously choose to release all that did not serve their soul and the callings of their heart.

One of life's ironies is that, when it comes to spiritual matters, 'knowing' is an individual experience. However, if the contents of this book strike a chord with the reader's heart and resonate deeply, it can become their reality.

Best wishes to the readers for embracing their liberating journey of life.

Is Your Mind really Yours?

1

DISCOVERING YOUR TRUE SELF

"To get to know who you truly are, you may need to reflect on who you are not.

"Once the realisation of who you really are sets in, you break down all the walls of an illusory existence.

Life opens up to a totally new dimension for us to experience freedom, growth and contentment.

Our 'naturalness' as children

Let's just step back in time and revisit the early years of growing up.

As infants, we had no idea of who we were. It's only many years later that we understood ourselves as having been vulnerable, free-spirited and loveable. We were tender, spontaneous, unpretentious, non-judgemental and above all, just being in the moment, in accordance with our true nature.

We innocently played with one another, were often energetically mischievous but blissfully ignorant of any 'differences' defined by religion, caste, skin colour, language, customs or economic status. We just accepted one another without any preconceived barriers or a tendency to affix tags of discrimination.

Yes, we experienced physical pain, were often restless, and would cry, but we were incapable of being stressed out or worried. Our parents just had to hold us in their arms and cuddle us, and we instinctively trusted them, knowing that all would be well with us. We did not comprehend the language of words but surely 'sensed' the language of love and warmly responded to it.

The start of 'mind programming' and development of belief structures

Our innate vulnerability as children made us totally dependent on our parents. We started to get pampered and have all our demands met 'on call'. Parents were ever at our service. We became the centre of attention. It was as if the entire world existed only to serve our needs. The planting of the seed that would germinate as the fabricated ego had already begun. The 'I', 'ME' and 'MINE' syndrome had already started playing out.

As we grew up, we were like a CD, waiting for a variety of songs to get recorded on it. The myriad songs would collectively represent the voices of our parents, teachers, relatives, friends and everyone we came in contact with. Each person had a role to play in injecting us with their respective ideas, expectations, 'rights' and 'wrongs' of life and in fact a whole set of viewpoints, seen from *their own* perspective of the world. We would also learn to erect barriers of separation from the outside world, compartmentalise people and label situations as 'good' or 'bad', depending on what was taught to us.

As a result, we grew up with a certain 'programming', a software loaded with the opinions of all and sundry. Then, as the interaction with our environment increased through exposure to society at large, books, magazines, print and electronic media, and the Internet, we started to accumulate more inputs. All of these resulted in the formation of belief systems that got deeply embedded in our minds. Thus, we started to believe, for instance, 'If I take a dip in the river Ganges, I will cleanse myself of all sins', 'The relationship between a mother-in-law and daughter-in-law can rarely ever be smooth' or 'Whatever is in my destiny will happen; I cannot change the course of my life' and so on.

In a sense, therefore, people and our external environment largely defined our belief system and our self-image. These 'acquired' beliefs were rarely subjected to our scrutiny and we made them the reality of our lives, even though they may have had no semblance of truth in them. Everything we saw, experienced, thought and felt was adapted to align with our belief structures.

> Thus, more often than not, our beliefs were actually mere perceptions of reality rather than REALITY.

Consequently, all our thoughts, emotions and behaviour started to be predominantly influenced by whatever belief systems lay stored in our sub-conscious minds. We use the term 'our minds', but truly speaking our minds largely belonged to society, not to us, isn't it? That's because the bulk of the implantation of viewpoints into our minds was done by society.

> The mind is society's garbage bin. Everyone who passes by stuffs something into it.
>
> —Sadhguru Jaggi Vasudev
>
> *Noted yogi, mystic and philanthropist*

Now, what happens as a consequence of this? If we have stored negative, limiting, constricting belief structures in our programmed minds, will we not experience those very negative and limiting situations in our lives? Why so? Because the job of the subconscious mind, which is non-judgemental, is simply to create the reality out of the various impressions, right or wrong, that lie stored in it. Therefore, we are more often than not, operating on autopilot mode. But that's one part of the issue; the other is that most of these beliefs are being played out in our lives, without us even being aware of it.

Suppose our programming is:

- 'As I am not fair-complexioned, I will not be able to attract a good-looking partner in my life.'
- 'I will be appreciated and accepted only if I conform to my parents'/teachers'/friends' way of thinking and behaving.'
- 'I am not capable or hardworking enough to clear the Engineering entrance examinations.'

We have already *chosen*, without realising it, the situations and circumstances we would encounter in our lives, as well as the habits and the manner in which we would respond to our environment. It is also an unfortunate fact that most of the programmes running in our subconscious minds have their roots in some form of negativity or the other, such as fear of rejection in a relationship, lacking confidence in ourselves, or worrying about what the future will have in store for us.

Mental conditioning: Leading to limitations and barriers to our rhythmic flow and progress

Since the mind is largely moulded and programmed by the external environment, we tend to operate from impulses and reflexes, constantly driven by people and situations. But how much say do we have in this? Pretty little, isn't it?

Your mind is thus conditioned to operate with a remote control that is not in your hands. It is this conditioning that tells you what to think, what to feel, and how to act and behave. It draws the boundaries of your imagination and creativity whilst predefining your limitations in terms of what you are capable of achieving. It does not allow you freedom to explore and discover your own reality about yourself and your environment beyond the confines of the boundaries drawn. This conditioning becomes your biggest barrier in letting you flow in the rhythm of life and being open to limitless possibilities for your growth. Would not being in such a situation make you feel like a caged parrot in bondage that is yearning to break free from the shackles of imprisonment and fly in freedom, in harmony with its own true nature?

> Now think about this: Can society, situations and circumstances hold power over you without your consent? You might agree that they can, only as long as you allow them to do so.

And that is the challenge—consciously choosing not to allow society to rule and run your life.

But here is the irony. We are quick to press the 'Delete' button on our computers when we want to rid it of all the garbage that doesn't serve our purpose. We do not hesitate in banishing these to the 'Trash' folder. But why don't we do the same to the garbage that lies in our minds, because a lot of what lies stored is not only trash but is actually pulling us down and hindering our growth? You might find that you do not drop limiting belief systems because you may start feeling lost, because you cannot exist in a vacuum, or because your identity may be compromised or rendered irrelevant. In fact, without a belief system you might wonder who you truly are.

The harmful and degenerative effects of societal conditioning can be mind-boggling. We just have to look at the world today, engulfed by feelings of hatred, violence, and strife, giving rise to a raging intolerance amongst different countries, religions, castes and sub-castes, each trying to denigrate the other. Isn't this an offshoot of the distorted belief systems that the world has been fed and the religious conditioning that has been hammered down, 'My religion is the only true religion', 'My caste is superior to all other castes' and so on? Such is the damaging influence of this conditioning that wars are being fought and violence is being increasingly perpetrated across the globe. Even educated youth are being radicalised and lured by some groups, through intensive conditioning, into resorting to brutality and merciless killing.

> We come to this world perfect with the signature of God. And then we are manipulated, contaminated, conditioned and pulled apart by human beings. And immediately our open sky starts closing, our windows, our doors start closing. We are no longer available to Existence. We become windowless. And that's our misery.
>
> —Osho
>
> *Indian mystic and spiritual teacher*

Your conditioning drives your thoughts and emotions

If you delve into your mind, you may agree it is nothing but a constant flow of thoughts. Observe your thoughts dispassionately and you will find that there is an endless chatter going on. The mind works overtime—judging, rationalising, worrying, dreaming, fearing, etc.—all of which is a consequence of your conditioning. So strong becomes the identification of ourselves with our thoughts that we mistakenly view the world from the prism of these thoughts. And isn't it a fact that we nurture thoughts, give them importance, attention and energy, pretty much like we pamper guests when they visit us? The more the attention we give to them, the more they stick to us. The more the attachment to the thoughts, the more we become a prisoner to them. Thoughts lead to desires and expectations to which we get attached while we also restlessly yearn for their fulfilment. And when these fail to materialise, we find ourselves reeling under stress, anxiety, frustration and despair.

Identification with the ego and its illusion: At the root of our problematic and caged existence?

The interaction of the physical body with our thoughts, emotions, beliefs and conditioning gave rise to the ego. This became our protective barrier that sought to reaffirm our identity with the outer world.

The common refrain when people come across the word 'ego' is: 'All of us have an ego. So what's the big deal?' Sure, we all have an ego and from one *limited* perspective, the ego is required for us to carry out our daily activities and actualise our individual aspirations. It is also a mechanism used for our protection and survival. But does the ego have any independent existence of its own? It can't, since it is purely a mental construct that has been fabricated.

But the ego considers itself real and relentlessly works, not just to establish control over our being but over others' as well. So subtle is the ego that it manifests itself moment by moment in our thoughts, words and actions. Its sole preoccupation is with its self-image (how we think and feel about ourselves) and the underlying emotions that have a bearing on that self-image, whether positively or adversely.

Would then ego be something that is inherently bad, as is most often believed?

Like anything in this world, 'good' and 'bad' are only tags conceived by the mind. In the context of the ego too, it is inherently neither bad nor good. All that is relevant is whether the ego is being used constructively for our overall growth or is using us in a manner that makes us subservient to its diktats and we allow it to sabotage our freedom and inner harmony.

> It is the **dysfunctional** aspect of the ego and the erroneous identification with it which ends up tormenting us and robbing us of our peace.

Here's how our identification with the ego can deeply affect us:

- **Inner restlessness**: Our identification with our physical bodies, thoughts and emotions becomes so deep-rooted that we are deluded into believing that these define us in totality, that there can be no further description of who we are.

In all our interactions with the world around us, are we not presenting ourselves in terms of our names, genders, family backgrounds, religions, castes, sects, educational qualifications, designations, achievements, material possessions, and various other tags and labels that get affixed onto us, along with a host of other embellishments? But all these only serve to give us an illusion of our individuality. Why the illusion? Simply because we have got stuck on a concept of self-importance. It's like presenting to the world a well-drafted CV or resume with our photograph. It is supposedly through this CV or passport that we get defined by the world. This is the ego at work, sending us false messages by masking our true nature, which does not depend on the 'outside' for any self-validation. Consider that my thought is: 'I am a high-flying CEO working with a very prestigious MNC. I earn a seven-figure salary with handsome bonuses and stock options to boast, whilst enjoying a most luxurious lifestyle.' Notice that I am not centred in my own being through this identity. I am at the mercy of changing circumstances (recession, competition, possible ill health, change in ownership of the enterprise, mergers, etc.) through which my exterior identity may be lost. If the job goes, my position is gone. Or if I retire, my status is gone. Now I struggle to find a fresh identity, and therein is my inner restlessness. This is the ego at work. It thrives on accentuating a sense of separateness not only from our original, authentic nature but also from the source of all creation and manifestation of divinity.

- **The mental struggle**: We no longer see the world as it is but from the lens of our distorted beliefs, from the 'tags' which falsely define us. Since the mind is constantly projecting itself, it interferes with reality, and that is why it sees only what it wants to see. This creates a problem for us in accepting people and circumstances as they are, and an inner struggle wages within our own being.
- **Non-peace**: So as to keep rearing its head, the ego resorts to one-upmanship and domination over those it comes into contact with. Where there is an intense need to dominate, control and be ever self-righteous in relation to others, there can be no room to love. Nor is an environment created for receiving love. When love is not received, the 'I' starts to experience frustration, agitation, and rejection. One gets into a state of despondency. One is not at peace with oneself.
- **Feeling of incompleteness**: The ego is always in a state of 'wanting', 'seeking' or 'fearing'. This is its compulsive preoccupation to keep itself alive and kicking. That is why it continuously drives one to seek the next level of gratification—a bigger house, a higher paying job, a swankier car, more luxuries, etc.—in the mistaken belief that these will complete it. But all it does is create a restless and agitated state of mind because it does not accept contentment. The mentally constructed false self is ever insecure because it has not gotten over the illusion of being in a state of 'lacking' and feeling 'incomplete'.

- **Jealousy and envy**: The ego is in a constant state of comparison. When it sees good things happening to others, or it finds someone who has more wealth or more knowledge or a better-looking partner, it feels belittled, and this gives rise to jealousy and envy. Now it needs to strengthen its diminished identity. How does it do this? By seeing itself as more unjustly treated by life than others. By complaining and reacting, it labels other people and situations as 'wrong' and itself as 'right' so that it can once again feel 'superior'.
- **Inner confusion and conflict**: The ego is a great master at creating inner confusion. This confusion is between the image we project to the world and what the heart feels. We often live in a make-believe world that is not in harmony with our spirit.

  There is confusion because we believe we are the image we project to the world, yet we also get a sense of something missing, something not quite right, some dissatisfaction. This is because we are not living authentic lives wherein we are true to ourselves.

  Driven by the ego operating from the dimension of 'separateness' and wishing to dominate and establish its superiority, we end up having conflicts, fears and misunderstandings in our relationships. The ego strengthens its identity by 'running down' others' views, beliefs, opinions and judgements whilst fiercely resisting situations and circumstances it labels as 'undesirable' or 'unpleasant'.
- **Denying our true potential**: We end up becoming a prisoner of our thoughts, denying, in the process, our true

potential, our own very dreams and aspirations. We accept mediocrity and limitations, and resign ourselves to our fate. While a part of us may want to break free, the hold on us by the conditioned mind is so powerful that we feel trapped and caged and seem incapable of taking on life's many challenges.

- **Anger and hostility**: The ego is a function of the thoughts that the mind preoccupies itself with. These thoughts evoke feelings, desires and expectations to which we get attached. Whenever a desire cannot be fulfilled or outcomes are not in line with our expectations, anger, frustration or hostility arises.

It would thus appear that practically all the 'lower order' life states of jealousy, arrogance, greed, pride, frustration, anger, doubt, worry, confusion, despair, isolation, etc. are rooted in the workings of the ego. Whether we admit it or not, we *all* have these lower order traits in us, just as we also have the higher order traits of love, compassion, peace, forgiveness, selflessness, and so on.

> What only matters is which of these traits surface and manifest at any given point in time during our interaction with the self and our external world.

Even though we mature as adults, many of us invariably carry with us inner conflicts that remain unresolved.

When we lead our lives under the control of the ego, we play out various roles in the theatre of life. Our interaction with the world is through the protective mask of the ego. And here's the rub: We may find ourselves wearing several masks depending upon whether we are interacting with our spouses, children, parents, relatives, seniors at the work place, etc. A strong identification with the various roles we play makes us oblivious to who we really are.

> With several masks to wear, we may wonder, 'Which is the real me?'

We get distanced from our true self and start gravitating towards conformity, the expectations of others, and ignoring what our hearts truly desire. We grow confused because we try to navigate our lives convincing our heads of something our hearts know to be a lie. But the ego does not allow us to drop our masks because it seeks an identity that needs to be projected as a differentiated, separate entity from the rest of the external world. And as we go on leading a life of delusion, we can no longer find joy or have harmonious relationships with ourselves and hence with the world we interact with.

Disillusionment, disenchantment and a sense of despair all follow because we have chosen to get attached to this *false* 'I', and are living a programmed existence where the programme is not totally ours but largely acquired from the outside world.

> When we realise that many of the beliefs we store in our minds and the thoughts we nurture may have no relevance whatsoever, we take the first step towards the mitigation of our misery.

Finding yourself: Who is the real you?

Surely we were not brought into this world to lead a life of misery. Nor was it intended that we continue to struggle with ourselves and remain confused. If the conditioned mind becomes the cause for our turmoil, there must be something else that makes for our true identity, which goes deeper and beyond the aggregate of our thoughts, perceptions, indoctrinations, experiences and memories. But the problem is that the subtle aspect of our real identity cannot be discerned by the mind, which is full of noise, clutter and all kinds of prejudices.

This then leads us to the question: Who really am I?

One thing is clear: I am *not* the ego—thoughts, feelings and emotions—since all of these are triggered and constructed by external factors. Moreover, thoughts and beliefs constantly change and have no permanence, so how can I be something that is always changing? Nor can I be the body, which is not just transient and perishable but only a vehicle for carrying out my worldly activities or discharging my roles. I also can't be my habits, since these too are an offshoot of my conditioning and can be broken. Then who am I?

The answer to this question is perhaps the toughest of all to construct and can only spring from within you when you delve deeper and go beyond the tags and impressions acquired from the external world. For such impressions have only ended up justifying the need for us to be judgemental, self-centred and ever in a state of want. Hence, the more we seek our identity from the outside world, the more we lead superficial lives and cannot explore the core of our true being to get to truly know ourselves.

But you can *direct your focus to the heart* and ask yourself some honest questions, such as:

What do *you* really want to do in life? What is *your* driving passion? What are *your* unique talents and strengths? What makes *you* feel unhappy, irritated, angry, fearful, insecure, etc.? Who are the people *you* feel drawn to and whom *you* wish to enter into a relationship with, and so on and so forth. In fact, many aspects can be intimately 'uncovered' about *you*.

Somewhere in the depths of your being, you may sense an inner voice answering your questions, communicating a certain feeling, sending out bodily sensations—all of which contain the cues and pointers of who you really are and what your spirit intends for you in your life's journey. But, chances are, you did not heed the voices because these were overpowered by the relentless chatter of your mind pulling you in different directions, depending on the programmes stored in your subconscious mind. But the subtle voices that sprung from within you were not part of any programming; they just arose because somewhere inside you there is an energy field, sending out signals to you. There was no logic required. The energy field simply communicated what it truly felt was the direction your life needed to take.

Can this energy field within you then be the real 'you', which is the abstract spirit, soul, or divinity having the physical body as its vehicle to carry out its mission (and not the body having a soul)? The mind or the ego is then only a 'drama' being played out—a drama that the mind mistakenly projects as reality. But this is because we are disconnected from the real source—the energy field or the soul, and for that matter even the heart, which just 'knows' and needs no reasoning.

What if you turn your attention inwards and connect with your inner being through a dis-identification with the mind/ego interplay?

Is it possible that there is an alternative way to live your life based on a superior intelligence that is unconditioned and uncontaminated? What if this intelligence was guiding you through the genuine sensations and feelings arising in your heart? What if you were now to align and harmonise your life with this divine energy and realise that the true essence of your being is love, from which all creation springs?

Being true to yourself: What does it entail?

You start to lead a life from the dimension of your true self when:

- You are just being YOU and not trying to become something or someone else.

Look at nature—does the eagle try to be like the dove or does the deer try to be like the lion? No.

Each being exists in accordance with its own nature and does its job of blossoming the only way it was intended to. Why must humanity choose to do what is not in alignment with what its soul or its true self has intended for it? Would it not be a feeling of great disillusionment to be someone other than yourself, or for that matter live by the expectations and norms of society?

But when you are being yourself, you no longer feel the need to interact with your world while wearing a mask and nurturing fears or worries of being 'exposed'.

- You go where your heart truly wishes to go and you don't need to do anything against your inner voice just to please others.

The mind, on its own, can never decipher the truth of your inner calling because of its programming. Listening to others means abandoning your own true dream—the one that only your heart 'knows' and guides you towards. You no longer feel the need for self-validation, for once you are aligned with the heart, there is no room for self-doubt. Your conviction stemming from your heart's voice is unshakeable. You consciously choose to follow *your* own dreams and not live out the dreams of others.

- You lovingly accept yourself as you are, even with all your imperfections and blemishes.

You realise that you are gifted, unique and special in your own way. Your imperfections don't come in the way of limiting your potential because you choose not to let these define you.

> You are original. You are rare. You are unique. You are a wonder. You are a masterpiece…your master's piece… Celebrate your uniqueness.
>
> —Sri Sri Ravishankar
> *Spiritualist and founder, Art of Living*

- You no longer feel the need to say 'yes' when your heart wants to say 'no'.

This is a situation many of us may have had to reckon with in the course of our life's journey. We feel we would end up hurting others if we were to say 'no' at times. In doing so, we do not live our lives with authenticity.

The reality is that by ignoring the true signals coming from the depths of our being, we only create for ourselves an inner disharmony, and that's no way to enjoy life, which is a rare gift given to us.

- You no longer need to conform to the expectations of society, but lead a life which is in accordance with the callings of your heart.

It's your life and your journey. It would be inconceivable to even remotely experience the fullness and richness of it if you live a life that conforms to the ideals of others. A life lived according to the template of others would surely be a life needlessly frittered away and wasted. Would not allowing others to serve as your benchmark keep you in bondage all your life? Isn't it akin to the feeling of a good part of you dying even while you are alive?

- You are no longer driven by the mind but choose instead to be in the driver's seat and guided by your inner voice.

You now direct your mind and channelise it in the direction which harmonises with your inner being. Thus, you don't let the mind run your life but you tell the mind what needs to be done.

Since it's almost impossible to blank out thoughts, you choose to sublimate the mind by shifting your thoughts from those that limit you and pull you down to those that uplift you. In your day-to-day life, moment to moment, you now make choices and take decisions that deeply resonate with the spirit within.

> What you think, feel, say and do are all in perfect consonance.
> You realise that you need nothing from the outside to complete you.

All that you seek from life is there within the recesses of your being—a space wherein there are limitless possibilities and potential for the creation of something of great value and growth, not just for yourself but for your environment. With your determination and the divine power to guide and support you, you can co-create your circumstances.

In this manner you become awakened to the reality that, whilst you have a mind, you are *not* the mind. Because if you identify with the mind, it is the mind that is using you. You can use the mind constructively only when you are aware that it is not a part of your core essence. As long as your identification is there with the mind, you are caught in its snare and it orders you around. So whether the mind will become the cause for your bondage or for your liberation (or whether the mind will be your master or you the master of the mind) is a choice you can empower yourself to make.

> Your burden is of false self-identifications. Abandon them all.
>
> —Nisargadatta Maharaj
> *Renowned Indian sage*

It is this de-identification with the mind/body and re-connection with the true self that can bring about radical shifts in your life's journey.

Just sense the difference you experience when you see yourself as a peaceful soul, with love as the essence of your being, having enormous potential for growth and realising your true aspirations.

Would you feel trapped or caged, caught within the prison of your mind's own making, if you had no boundaries drawn, no set belief systems to limit you, but an ocean of opportunities available to you when you operate from the perspective of your soul and its calling?

> Would you not feel free in the real sense if you broke away from the shackles of the programming that does not allow you to be who you truly are, but what the world expects you to be?

Life's journey can be liberating—by choosing to live, in awareness, from the true self rather than from the egoistic or fictional self.

Let's accept one thing. Your life is your choice. You have chosen it with your belief systems. Irrespective of how you have viewed your life and lived it so far, the comforting submission is:

> YOU have the choice to align with your true self and experience an immensely liberating journey.

This liberating journey starts when you trust your own heart to re-examine many of the beliefs you have blindly accepted without questioning. Beliefs that do not serve a purpose in your journey need to be dropped by the wayside. You then make fresh determinations and set goals that are aligned with your true callings. Your life is now your own. There is no one responsible for its quality but you. You are no longer attached to the thought of whether or not you will reach your destination; you just begin to enjoy every moment of the journey, like a bird that just spreads its wings and experiences the joy of flying.

Thus, at any point of your life, you will always have a choice.

> To operate from the fictional self and the workings of the mind/ego, which creates disturbance.
>
> OR
>
> To operate from the true self, which leaves you more at peace with yourself.

Of course, easier said than done, because the vexing problem is: How do you distinguish between the fictional self or the ego and the true self? The reality is that there is invariably a conflict raging within you, between your spirit, which is authentic, led by the heart, and the over-analytical programmed and contaminated mind. Since both seem persuasive enough, there will be moments when you experience a state of well-being and inner calmness whilst at some other moment you could be in a turmoil, gripped by the workings of the ego. In fact, more often than not, you may wonder where the true self is when you are feeling depressed or facing crises and difficult circumstances. This is because habits of a lifetime are not easy to reprogramme and call for persistence of your sincere efforts to change them.

However, with time and practice, you get to discriminate between choices that result from the 'voices' of your inner self that create a deep, comforting resonance of affirmation within you, and choices that are an offshoot of your biases, prejudices and judgements coming from the ego, which more often than not would be out of synch with your own truth.

The 'guiding light' of the inner true voice will always ensure that you live an authentic, contented life. When it conflicts with the voice of the ego, wisdom would suggest following the voice of the true self rather than being swayed by the trappings of the programmed mind.

And finally, some encouraging words that really strike a deep chord:

> Your time is limited, so don't waste it living someone else's life. Don't be trapped by dogma—which is living with the results of people's thinking. Don't let the noise of other's opinions drown out your own inner voice. And most importantly have the courage to follow your heart and intuition. They somehow already know what you truly want to become. Everything else is secondary.
>
> —Steve Jobs
>
> *Co-founder and former chairman/CEO of Apple Inc.*

∞

2

YOUR RELATIONSHIP WITH YOURSELF

"How can we delegate the job of liking ourselves to others?
That's got to be our responsibility, isn't it?

"Living lives of conformity and trying to please others may give them a high. But the point is—by not being ourselves and not living our own lives, can we ever be comfortable with our own selves?

Your relationship with yourself: What is it all about?

We live in a world characterised by interactions at various levels. As a result, we get enmeshed in several relationships—with our spouses, families, children, friends, colleagues, and so on. We spend quite some time and effort nurturing these relationships because they are important to us.

But let's think about this: How often do we reflect on the relationship we nurture with our own selves and with the situations and circumstances we encounter in our lives? We may wonder at the meaning and relevance of such a relationship with ourselves—so accustomed are we to view relationships with our external world. Moreover, implicit in the aspect of any relationship is the premise that there are two distinct identities relating to each other. But since we consider ourselves as one entity, the obvious question that arises is: How can one entity relate to itself?

In reality, the 'you' is the core or your true self—the very essence of your being, which is ever in a relationship with 'yourself', which is your mind and body. However, most of us tend to identify only with the mind and body, being unaware of the existence of the self. So here is something you may wish to honestly introspect on:

> Would it not be correct to say that more than with the external world, we perhaps spend most of our time with ourselves—with our thoughts, feelings and emotions?

Having a relationship with ourselves simply means being aware of how we perceive ourselves—our strengths, flaws, beliefs, physical bodies, goals and aspirations, the constant flow of all our thoughts and emotions, and, in fact, the reality of all that motivates us in our life's journey.

The bedrock of this relationship is how intimate, open and honest we are with ourselves and the degree of comfort we feel in this interaction with ourselves. After all, regardless of what goes on outside of us, whatever we experience—our joys, failures, frustrations, victories, etc.—is all happening inside of us. So it is the 'inside' where the seeds of any relationship with the 'outside' are nurtured.

Why is a relationship with yourself so critical?

We all understand that our external world is just a mirror reflecting the state of our internal world. Hence, a relationship with ourselves will ultimately determine how people relate to us and how we choose to respond to all the circumstances we will encounter. If, for instance, we see ourselves as incompetent, lacking in confidence, insecure, etc. then we send out vibrations that are picked up by the antenna of the universe and we will tend to attract people, circumstances and events in our lives to support this self-image. The same is also true if we carry positive perceptions about ourselves. Without a healthy self-image, our efforts to grow and be successful in all spheres of life are unlikely to bear fruit.

When you think about it, many things—be it your mission and goals, achievements and growth, inner contentment, and in fact your state of mind—depend on your ability to connect with your true self.

The uncomfortable truth, however, is that while most of us are adept at evaluating how other people act and behave, very few of us have any inclination to introspect and observe our own thoughts and behaviours. In the course of our lives, we tend to acquire an ideal self-image about who and what we should be. When the gap between this desired self-image and the one that is the current reality is wide, we struggle with ourselves, there is a sense of inner turmoil, and peace eludes us. It is also a fact that many people find it uncomfortable to accept themselves with their flaws and invariably look for approval and validation from others. This is nothing but a manifestation of not having a healthy relationship with oneself.

Let's think about the following:

> Can you really have a fulfilling relationship with others if you do not firstly accept and love yourself as you are, even with all your imperfections?

This is a critical aspect. Can you really love others until you first find love within yourself? After all, you can give to others only what you have in the first place. When you love yourself, the world 'senses' these loving vibrations your persona exudes and responds lovingly. On the other hand, if we belittle ourselves and have a low sense of self-worth, are we not likely to find acceptance and love elusive?

So, how's the relationship with yourself?

Caught in the quagmire of chores, goals to be achieved, deadlines to be met, loose ends to be tightened and all the hustle and bustle of daily living, it would seem natural not being in a position to conduct a 'scan' of our inner world. The 'viruses' we carry keep showing up and problems surface in our relationships, be it on the home front, friends, society at large, or at the work place. In short, our 'system' crashes. We are quick to blame the external world for our troubled relationships, and this does not help our cause.

Before we blame others with whom our relationship is not working, let's ask ourselves: Is my relationship with myself really working? If not, then we may need to sort it out. It's a case to be cured and not endured.

All it takes is a few minutes off from your busy schedule to have an honest dialogue with the self—a calm contemplation of the nature and source of your emotions and feelings. This self-awareness can only come about by delving deep within. It is a vital step in helping us decode where our thoughts, emotions, beliefs, and our interpretations of them, are leading us in our journey. In the process, we may understand that whether or not our journey of life will be fulfilling would depend on what belief systems we carry and where we choose to focus our attention and energies. We may realise that, through a change of mindset by making the shift from uncomfortable, disturbing thoughts and emotions we nurture, we can have dramatic and positive changes in our personality and state of well-being, leading to a changed reality.

The key question that you may then reflect on is:

> Are you not much better off channelising your energies fixing your relationship with yourself before trying to fix the world?

Because the fact is that trying to fix the world without any inner transformation will be an exercise in futility.

Choosing from contrasting mindsets: Directing your life in a positive flow

The great beauty of life is that it *always* presents us with a choice between:

> Holding onto mindsets and thoughts that will be counter-productive to our peace, well-being, growth and freedom.
>
> OR
>
> Redirecting our attention and energy to mindsets and thoughts that would be regenerative and make the journey of life fulfilling.

You may find that the former perspective has its roots in the workings of the conditioned mind as the 'driver' of your being, whereas the latter perspective is rooted in your free spirit directing your mind. What you focus on is what you attract. It follows that paying proper attention to the qualities of your thoughts assumes a lot of importance. Our thoughts constitute the creative force in our lives.

Your energy will go where your thoughts go. So, if you harbour worry, resentment, guilt, fear, etc., what happens? As you think negative thoughts about undesirable outcomes, you are actually giving energy to and inviting the very circumstances you would not want in your life. You may not even be consciously aware of the role you would have played in experiencing such circumstances. No wonder, then, that almost all of our sufferings is a consequence of the thoughts that we allow to enslave us.

The following set of contrasting states of mind may be worth thinking upon. If any mindset creates disharmony and inner turbulence and you find yourself becoming a prisoner of such states, it may be time for you to let go of these and make the shift to more positive and life-enhancing mindsets.

> Which of these mindsets you go with is thus a matter of your conscious choice.

Low self-confidence and low self-esteem *vs* self-acceptance and healthy self-worth

Your self-esteem is simply the overall opinion you have about yourself. It is a function of all the beliefs you hold and the experiences you went through right from your childhood, including the messages you received from everyone you interacted with. Consciously or unconsciously we turn these opinions to the reality of our lives. So, harbouring many self-defeating thoughts (I am incapable, I am not loveable, etc.) that we may have been programmed with, often results in low levels of self-esteem, self-worth and confidence. In the process, without even being aware, we may cause immense pain and damage to ourselves. We become fearful of 'exposing' ourselves to the world lest we are denied acceptance by them. So, to keep boosting its morale and shaking off any insecurity, the ego yearns for validation. This becomes the biggest barrier for us to pursue our dreams and aspirations.

> Having a low opinion of yourself is not modesty. It is self-destruction. Holding your uniqueness in high regard is not egotism. It's a necessary pre-condition to happiness and success.
>
> —Dr Bobbe Sommer
>
> *Leading psychotherapist and author*

However, since it is your thoughts which impact your self-esteem, by a shift in your thoughts you could move away from the debilitating syndromes of low self-esteem.

> To start with, what if you accept yourself as you are?

Self-acceptance is about being totally at ease with who you are. It means not struggling with or feeling guilty about certain aspects of your personality that you have judged as aberrations. However, self-acceptance does not imply that you have to resign yourself to your fate and believe that that there is nothing you can do to transform yourself. When you accept yourself as you are, you take the first vital step in bringing about changes and transformations in your inner self. You accomplish this not by judging and belittling yourself but simply by being aware of your current behavioural patterns, habits and personality traits that you do not feel comfortable about. You then choose to bring about changes as you deem fit, not because there is a demand on you to do so by others.

In the process, you enhance your self-worth, so you can carry conviction in your capabilities, not just when things are going your way but even when the chips are down. An elevated self-worth gives you the confidence to navigate your life's journey without doubts and fears. You no longer feel the need to compare yourself to others and their achievements or to rely on them for your happiness.

You are your own 'icon'. It's about loving yourself and embracing the unique 'you' and your value-creating potential, not just for yourself but for others as well.

> You realise that, while society may pass value judgements on you, they may not always be fair in doing so, because even if they know what all you have been through, they do not know how you feel deep within your heart.

Seeking validation from others *vs* trusting oneself with conviction

Here's a candid submission for consideration: Is it not a fact that many of us carry an opinion about ourselves based on what perceptions others hold about us? Is it also not true that we often act in certain ways, dress up in particular styles and pursue goals of a kind that get us the stamp of approval from others so that we are not branded as 'losers' or 'laggards'? *You might agree that we do care a lot about others' opinions.*

Perhaps we have been conditioned to seek the approval and validation of others. Like it or not, it is *we* who give others the power to define us.

Someone doesn't appreciate my new dress or hairstyle and I wonder whether my sense of fashion is really up to it. My boss does not value or appreciate my contribution to the assignment at the workplace and I get hurt, disappointed, perhaps even angry. I develop an inferiority complex and wonder whether 'I am really worth it'.

Why do we attach so much importance to other's perceptions of us? Sure, it's natural to want to be appreciated, but are we saying that we cannot be fine unless those around us give us their favourable verdict? Each time we let others dictate our opinions about ourselves we get into a self-made trap that limits our growth and freedom.

Now, what if we were to change the content of the 'internal communication' that seeks constant dependency on other's validation to one which recognises and respects one's self-belief?

> What if I were to change my frequency to one that tells me: 'I am fine as I am and I don't need anyone's permission to feel so'.

The key to this change is the awareness that comes by simply being an observer and watching in a detached manner the deeply entrenched beliefs that give rise to self-defeating messages. Once I am aware, I can reprogramme my internal communication and with persistence develop conviction. This conviction respects my uniqueness, my perspectives, and my preferences, and I no longer feel the need to please all and sundry. There is now the realisation that having to change oneself just to get acceptance from others would mean that I am not liked for being 'me' but liked only when I conform. I no longer feel the need to compare myself with others and their achievements. It's about loving myself and embracing the unique 'me'.

> Because one believes in oneself, one doesn't try to convince others. Because one is content with oneself, one doesn't need others' approval. Because one accepts oneself, the whole world accepts him or her.
>
> —Lao Tzu
> *Ancient Chinese philosopher*

In the final scheme of things, what only matters is the opinion I carry about myself, and how much trust I place in my own conviction. I can make a resolve to not be dictated by others. It's quite possible that I may not be liked by some for not towing their line. So be it. I am not in a popularity contest. The people who genuinely love me will do so for who I am, and that's what matters. Rather than harbour feelings of self-doubt, I take recourse to my inner voice to guide me in terms of what I want from life.

> Why not therefore cut the umbilical cord of attachment to the validation of others? This very moment. After all,
> it's YOUR self-worth at stake.

A sense of deprivation *vs* having gratitude

The mindset stemming from the egoistic self is ever in a state of 'wanting', fuelled by a perception of 'lack'. It would thus appear natural that under this misguided illusion, we complain about a whole lot of desirable things and situations missing in our lives. Where is my focus? On what I don't have. What is my signal to the universe / existence / the infinite intelligence? One of being deprived. So what does the universe do? It simply perpetuates this state of 'deprivation' and I feel trapped and helpless in this vicious cycle I have created.

> But what if I could redirect my focus on all that I am blessed with and sincerely (not just by my words but a deep feeling) express my gratitude to the divine powers (within me)?

When I realise that this alignment with the true self connects me to the powers through which I can obtain what I seek, I do not feel trapped but empowered. The more I live in gratitude, the more positive vibes I radiate and the more fulfilling experiences I encounter. This sets in motion a continuous offering of gratitude by me and receiving of blessings in various forms from the universe. In fact, I can cultivate a habit of having gratitude for almost everything that comes my way, because all of it contributes towards my advancement.

Playing the victim *vs* taking responsibility

Is it not common to come across people who believe in blaming all and sundry for their problems, setbacks, disappointments and misfortunes? If my boss at work is displeased with my performance and gives me an unsatisfactory report card or denies me a promotion, he / she is branded as one who is unfair, insensitive or partial to other colleagues.

If I am criticised for something I have done and feel hurt or angry, I quickly get into the 'poor me' syndrome and seek support from people who will reinforce the impression as to how unjustly I was treated.

The resulting emotional state of a victim is one of self-pity, which leads to frustration, despair, insecurity and even a repressed state of anger. But why do people get to play the victim card? As various studies by psychologists reveal, the origins of a victim mentality can be linked back to childhood, wherein people could have been denied love, affection, security and other positive strokes. They could have been unduly criticised and reprimanded, whether by parents, teachers, relatives or friends. Some of these children later grow up lacking in self-confidence, having unresolved emotions and feeling incapable of coming to terms with the world.

Further, the ego defence mechanism comes into active play and projects a feeling of having been 'wronged', with people, situations and circumstances labelled as the 'culprit' for our failures. We disown responsibility and think 'nothing is right with the world' and the feeling of 'why do I have to suffer for no fault of mine?' becomes dominant.

Playing the role of a victim can be very self-defeating. Since the inherent tendency is to make others the culprit for all that is going wrong with us, there is no room for self-reflection and self-correction. As such, victims continue to remain rooted in states of hopelessness and despair with a low self-image. Their relationship with the world remains unhealthy since their focus remains only on their miserable state. Moreover, they tend to manipulate people to get attention and love, using 'self-pity' as the tool to do so. Since no one likes to be manipulated, relationships usually end up being very superficial and hence the cycle of being a victim is relentlessly perpetuated.

So how do we free ourselves from the victim mode?

It calls for a shift in mindset wherein we take responsibility for our thoughts, emotions and actions.

Furthermore, the 'shift' takes place when we begin to realise that playing the blame game or offering excuses for all problems that come our way will not serve our purpose. The only thing we may end up doing is giving up our power to bring about an inner transformation. It's not going to be an easy job enhancing our life, but it's going to be impossible to do so if we don't take personal responsibility for it. Patience, courage, unwavering commitment and tenacity of purpose are the ingredients required to transform ourselves. It may seem a tall order, but once the determination is made to change from within, the 'inner' revolution will follow for sure.

> It is not uncommon for someone to be a self-saboteur and compound that by also having a victim mentality. It is as though they are holding their own breath and then blaming others for their own inability to breathe. If they can break free from this cycle, everything in their life changes for the better.
>
> —Dr Steve Maraboli
>
> *Speaker, bestselling author and behavioural scientist*

Loneliness *vs* aloneness

In the fast-paced, self-centred times that we live in, loneliness is not just confined to singles, widowers, divorcees and senior citizens, but is prevalent even amongst married couples and teenagers.

'Loneliness' and 'aloneness' are often used synonymously, but isn't there a difference between the two?

In loneliness, we have not befriended ourselves and are invariably seeking something or someone to fill an inner vacuum. There is a compelling need to cling to and depend on others so as to overcome our sense of insecurity and personal discomfort. But think about this:

> Can a lonely person ever give anything to a relationship?

In seeking others, aren't we using them just to fill up a void? The other person is not important but merely an instrument to be manipulated.

That is why, when we choose loneliness, we choose dependency and non-love and get into a vicious circle from which there is no escape:

Loneliness → Dependency → Exploitation → Lack of Love

(Lack of Love →) No relationship (→ Loneliness)

> The worst loneliness is not to be comfortable with yourself.
>
> —Mark Twain
>
> *Noted American writer*

Aloneness, however, can be very liberating. There is a sense of freedom because there is no dependency or exploitation of one's insecurities and vulnerabilities. There is a harmonious relationship with our inner selves and there is no need to run away from ourselves because we have befriended our own being. In aloneness we create space for unleashing our creativity and passion in whatever form it may be. We see ourselves not as isolated entities, but as part of a whole—a manifestation of divinity, which is always connected with us in our 'aloneness'.

Many would, however, argue that if humans by nature are social animals, they need the company of others. So why this big fuss about reaching out to others as an antidote to loneliness? Sure, we all need to reach out to others and it's perfectly fine and healthy to do so, but the crux is:

> Are we reaching out to just use others as a means to escape from our loneliness or are we reaching out because the love that resides within us needs an expression to be shared with others?

If we befriend others so as to escape from our inherent loneliness, it would not take long for cracks to develop in our relationships and we would be back to square one.

The fact of the matter is that one can be lonely even in a crowd and be alone and yet not lonely. Embracing one's aloneness and being totally comfortable with it can go a long way in creating a more lively, effusive YOU, bubbling with vitality.

> You are now operating from your true self and not the compulsions of the ego. People are drawn to you, and cultivating deep ties of genuine and warm friendships becomes the focus rather than just having friends around you.

Holding grudges *vs* forgiveness

In the course of our interactions with the world, many of us may have at some time or the other experienced a feeling of being unfairly let down, hurt, insulted or even cheated. There could have been instances where people may have reneged on their promises or commitments.

So, what was our natural reaction? Well, we invariably held on to the hurt, harboured feelings of bitterness and kept carrying those grudges. But did this help us? At the end of it all, we were the ones that were experiencing a troubled state of mind. It was our peace that was being robbed. Clearly, it was an undesirable state to be in, for holding on to grudges and bitterness only ended up adversely impacting our total well-being (mental, physical and emotional) and the quality of our relationships with others.

Moreover, at a deeper level, we may understand that people who hurt us are not 'bad' but they are behaving the way they do because they are unaware of being ruled by their tendencies, which they have not overcome. So, what if we shifted away from this state and chose forgiveness instead? Clearly, forgiveness does not mean that we have condoned the other person's act or behaviour if it was intended to hurt us. It's just that we choose to forgive for our own sake, for our own sense of well-being, for our own peace rather than for the other. It's about letting go of the burden we carry and releasing what was undermining both our physical and mental health. Do we also need to forget the experience so that it does not torment us? The only thing we may wish to remember is the lesson we learnt from that experience—in terms of how it contributed to our growth.

> To forgive is to set a prisoner free and discover that the prisoner was you.
>
> —Lewis B. Smedes
> *Renowned theologian and author*

Attachment *vs* detachment

Attachment is something we all accept as a natural part and parcel of life. We get attached to our parents, life partner, children, family, friends, and for that matter to our domestic help and even pets. But that's not where it ends. We get attached to our material possessions, status, power, houses, wealth, beliefs, ideologies, regrets, fears, pain, pleasure and above all the plethora of desires that we harbour and await the fulfilment of.

Now, isn't that one colossal burden we carry? A little self-reflection would possibly tell us that everything we attach ourselves to is actually impermanent. But we give them a lot of importance, as if they are all that matter in life. Sure, material luxuries, status and fame give us a 'high' and make us feel great, but isn't that all momentary? Here's something to reflect on:

> Isn't this attachment, which is nothing but the play of the ego programmed to 'cling' and not be free, the root cause of our misery?

Such is the power of the ego that it creates an endless chain of cravings, waiting to be fulfilled. Ironically, it seems that the more we get, the more empty we feel, because there is always an operating force trying to 'pull' towards us more of everything that is transient.

So the feeling of 'something missing' despite all acquisitions still persists. Furthermore, it is also a fact that through a fierce attachment to all that you acquire, you also develop fears and worries about the possibility of losing them some time in the future.

Is it a surprise then that we end up experiencing stress and unease whilst messing up our present? Think about this: We attach ourselves to all that is fleeting—people come and go, and so do wealth and possessions; situations constantly undergo a change and don't last. Then why do we wonder why our happiness doesn't last?

Against the above backdrop our scriptures and spiritual masters talk about the need for detachment so as to realise a sense of contentment and peace. Rightly so. But detachment as a state of mind is often misconstrued.

> Detachment would imply valuing all that you have and loving all your near and dear ones, **without** getting enmeshed in a manner that you become obsessively possessive of all that is temporary in nature. While you continue to own things, you don't let things own you or consume you.

What detachment does *not* mean is giving up or renouncing material possessions and comforts, or disengaging ourselves from relationships. Nor do we have to give up desires, for even the need to give up desires would be a desire, isn't it? Moreover, desires are also necessary for our growth.

Detachment is about being in total awareness of the futility of equating contentment, peace and fulfilment with materialistic gains and everything that comes with a limited shelf life. The key question we need to ask ourselves is: Are our desires ruling and controlling us or are we the masters of our desires? When desires bind us through our ruthless attachment to them, they only end up manifesting in the form of turbulent, agitated and restless minds that drive us to degenerative and often derogatory acts. These are self-destructive and harmful to others. But desires directed and channelised in a responsible, constructive and value-creating manner can bring about enriched lives not just for ourselves but for fellow beings as well.

It is not easy to live normal lives with detachment. But for a moment if we move away from our programming and ask ourselves:

> Will I feel comfortable and enjoy being in a relationship with someone who wants to fiercely possess me or constantly cling to me, denying me my own space?

An honest answer might then convince us why attachment may not be a very liberating experience.

Building a robust relationship with yourself is a lifelong journey

Learning, as is rightly said, is a continuous process. It never ends. In that sense it's a journey rather than a destination. We continue to learn new aspects about ourselves through the aggregate of our experiences and interactions. Consequently, building a robust relationship with yourself is going to be a continuous journey as well. By no means is it going to be easy, but you may find it well worth it because, at every moment, you have the potential for making peace with yourself and for rising further in the evolutionary curve of your growth. When you open up the 'window blinds' of your life, you create ample space to attract healthy and fulfilling relationships with yourself, other people, and all the situations and circumstances that come your way.

It will take a lot of effort and a constant introspection through self-dialogue, but nurturing a robust relationship with yourself could perhaps be the most rewarding and fulfilling journey of your life.

∞

3

YOUR RELATIONSHIP WITH YOUR CIRCUMSTANCES

“We often tend to treat circumstances and situations in our lives as if they had a separate identity, a character of their own and an independent existence. But isn't all the meaning of whatever we encounter in our lives given only by our mind?

“Situations in life arise out of a complex interplay of universal forces and a divine intelligence at work. The human mind may not always be able to fathom or decode these. So would it not make sense to accept situations for what they are and only choose our response to them?

The essence of a relationship with your circumstances

From the moment we are born till we breathe our last, we are always encountering situations, events and circumstances in the external world that deeply impact us. Like the ebb and flow of a tide, we experience both 'highs' and 'lows', though many of us might feel that the 'lows' seem to have a longer shelf life.

> A little reflection might suggest that in the ultimate scheme of things, our inner struggle with what we encounter and hence our life condition is a function of the perceived 'gap' between:
> This is the way my life is.
> AND
> This is the way I want my life to be.

As long as there is no such gap and circumstances are perceived as 'favourable', I have a sense of well-being and happiness. However, the moment circumstances are 'unfavourable' and I sense a gap, despair sets in and instead of experiencing a happy state, an inner turmoil rages. The more the gap, the more I get removed from experiencing a state of joy and wellness, and the more is my suffering.

So it would appear that the benchmark for my happiness or suffering is governed by whatever goes on outside of me.

But let's think about this: Does any situation, circumstance or event have any inherent power to determine our life state? Are situations not intrinsically neutral in nature? Are they not just phenomena arising out of the workings of universal laws? Isn't it we who choose to give them power by our conditioned thoughts and interpretations? There would be a temptation to rebut this submission and argue from experience as to how it is practical not to get carried away or be affected by, say, a situation where we lose our jobs, get divorced or lose a loved one.

Sure, the events happening outside of us would undoubtedly *influence* our life state, but here's something to reflect on: Do they necessarily have to *determine* our life condition?

> The reason circumstances need not determine our life condition is that we can choose not to give them power through our conditioned interpretations and preoccupations with them.

As you face challenges and problems practically on a daily basis, you may feel 'consumed' by their magnitude and complexity. Your inability to face these challenges may give rise to a feeling of despair, which perhaps makes you feel that *everything* in life is controlled by a force outside of you—whether it is by the planets, like some may conclude, or just the forces of your destiny playing out.

There is the thought and there is the situation. Thinking about the situation and affixing a label 'good' or 'bad' on it, as if it had an identity of its own, is what our mind usually does. But nothing in this world that happens is at its core good or bad, isn't it? It just is. It is neutral. But when we judge it and give it a meaning, we are likely to get strayed from the 'factual' position and distort our reality. As such we remain trapped in an illusion of our own making. Let's say a business flounders (situation) and we start thinking 'I wonder whether I will ever be able to achieve financial prosperity' (an emotional reaction). Now where is the attention? Only on the emotional reaction, which we have made the reality of our life. With this response we would feel incapable of taking any concrete measures to get our business back in shape and our 'hopeless' situation only keeps getting accentuated.

> Is it not then prudent to infer that the main cause of our disturbed state of mind is hardly the situation but our thoughts about the situation?

However, if we disconnect our thoughts from the situation, and are aware only of the thoughts without having to judge them, we could take an appropriate set of empowering actions to breathe new life into our business. In a nutshell, therefore, what relationship you *consciously choose* to have with your set of circumstances is what will govern your entire life state.

You create your own life condition—your choice of thoughts shapes what you get to experience

Everything that happens in our world (every event, every circumstance) is based on an all-pervading principle of 'cause' and 'effect'. Every cause must produce an effect and every effect that we experience must have an underlying cause behind it. This principle is clearly validated by the manner in which the universe and nature function and hence cannot be doubted, whether it's the force of gravity causing objects to fall to the earth, or even something as simple as indigestion caused by overeating.

Once we accept this premise, it would follow that our present moment must be a consequence of all our choices exercised in the past. Moreover, the causes encompass not just the actions we performed but even the thoughts that we nurtured. After all, everything begins with a thought, the seeds of which along with our beliefs and emotions germinate to give us a resulting set of experiences. As such, when we make choices, we need to be aware that those choices are actually making our lives.

> We are what our thoughts have made us; so take care about what you think. Words are secondary. Thoughts live; they travel far.
>
> —Swami Vivekananda
>
> *Spiritual leader and founder, Ramakrishna Mission*

In other words, whatever frequency of inner vibrations, governed by our mental and emotional state we tune into (the 'cause'), will invite the same vibrations, which are nothing but the circumstances or experiences (the 'effect') we will encounter.

Take the case of two employees, both of whom happen to lose their jobs in a company downsizing program. One harbours feeling of despair and starts to believe: 'Now what will happen to my career? How will I meet the growing expenses and support my family? I have no reserves to fall back on'. In short, he displays a feeling of helplessness that becomes the cause for his suffering.

The other takes this development in his stride, accepts reality and thinks: 'This is just another milestone in my professional journey. Change is inevitable. Maybe there is something positive in losing my job, because the next assignment in another company, which is surely waiting for me, would lead to greater advancement and growth'. With this line of thinking and confidence in himself, this person proactively takes steps to find an alternative opening, and is able to do so because his focus is on a solution, backed by an implicit faith in the workings of the universal laws.

So it can't be the situation that causes anguish to a person, because the same situation may not bother another person who chooses to interpret and respond to the situation differently.

> Could we not then infer that suffering is actually 'manufactured' in the mind, which has chosen to be a victim? And who is the one suffering? Isn't it the ego? Since the ego is a mirage, don't we suffer more in our imagination than in reality?

What if we were to shift our thought patterns and realise that we *do* have the choice to create our own experiences and circumstances?

What if we were to become aware that it is not the nagging, demeaning boss at the workplace, an irritating, ever-demanding partner or failure in an exam that serves to make us unhappy? We may realise that the actual cause for our suffering lies within us because we have chosen to focus our thoughts on the situation, which we label as 'hopeless'.

> Would it thus not be right to conclude that the biggest barrier to our happiness is simply our belief that we are a 'hapless victim' and a 'handicapped' prisoner of our circumstances, succumbing to the vagaries of events happening outside of us?

How can anyone else be responsible for our misery? It's all about blaming no event, no situation, no person for our life condition. It's about taking total personal responsibility by first dropping negative thoughts about situations and then redirecting the mind towards seeking solutions in the firm conviction that there is no situation that cannot be transformed to experience an inner calmness.

But let's admit it—this is not always an easy job because we are primarily ruled by relentless mental conditioning and stored-up negative energies. Once we become aware of what thoughts create positive value for us, through sheer persistence we can get into the habit of energising only those thoughts that will catalyse positive life conditions for us.

That's not to say that we may still not experience problems in our lives. Realistically speaking, these may be inevitable, but 'to suffer' or 'not to suffer' is a choice we can always exercise.

But do we really exercise our choices in life out of free will?

The debate between free will and fate has been endless. It has always been about one at the exclusion of the other. At one end of the spectrum you have rationalists, who say 'We are the makers of our own destiny' and that we are free to exercise our choices in life. After all, many of us choose our professions, life partners, hobbies, etc. At the other end of the spectrum, we have fatalists, who declare 'Not a leaf stirs without the will of the Divine Grace', suggesting that we have no control whatsoever in our destiny, that we are mere puppets playing out a preordained script as per His will.

Now, let's think about this: Is it really a binary aspect in the sense that only one or the other position can be reality? We live a life that is characterised by the interplay of a complex set of forces, experiences and phenomena that are so multi-dimensional that it would be too simplistic to believe in only one position.

Moreover, if you think about it, accepting the existence of only free will or fate, but not both, makes the issue very perplexing for us. This is because if we accept that everything in life is preordained, we are left with a feeling of helplessness. Being tossed around by the forces of the universe without a sense of self-purpose and achievement through attainment of personal goals can be very frustrating. On the other hand, if we believe that the unfolding of our lives is totally a function of our free will, we are again left confused when we encounter events and experience outcomes without our say in them.

So here's a thought: What if we regard fate as events and situations that will come our way at a given point in time (which may be quite outside our control) and consider free will to be about choosing how we respond to what we encounter? The renowned spiritual leader, Sri Ramakrishna Paramhansa, had an interesting analogy to offer. According to him, man is like a cow tied to a pole with a rope, bound by his karmic debts and human nature. The amount of free will he has is analogous only to the amount of freedom the rope allows. This analogy accepts the simultaneous existence of fate or determinism (what life will give to you) and free will (how you respond to what you get).

However, exercising one's free will is in itself not quite a simplistic matter. As we have seen earlier on, it is the sum total of all impressions stored in our subconscious minds that governs the way we think, feel and act. Thus, free will itself will come under the influence of our conditioning and programming.

> The term 'free will' implies that one is free to exercise one's choices voluntarily. But, as we have seen, we are so deeply conditioned by our upbringing, beliefs and experiences that our actions are usually driven by our innate tendencies and the messages the programmed mind relays to us. So there is hardly any volition herein.

As a consequence, we are often deluded into believing that we are the ones in total charge of all our decisions, whereas in truth it is largely our 'installed' programming, comprising our inherent tendencies and beliefs, that dictate our behaviour and actions.

So if we were to react to circumstances, driven by an impulse, would that be a free choice exercised? Can't be. If someone is rude to me, the defence mechanism of my ego activates itself, pretty much like the operating system of my programming, to give it back to him. Another person, however, operating from awareness, understands that the person abusing him must be waging an inner struggle with himself and, in empathy, chooses to ignore the abuse by not reacting. Thus, we can see that in the latter case there is an aspect of the person's consciousness that is simply aware in the moment, where the ego or conditioned mind is not the driver and the choice not to react has been made freely.

Thus, the more people believe in fate, that they have no freedom to exercise their choice, that *everything* is already predetermined, the more they limit themselves and remain bound by this belief.

> The pertinent question to ask therefore is: 'Are we puppets of fate or are we puppets of our conditioning and our impulses?'

We have the freedom to choose which thoughts and feelings to direct our attention and energy to. We are in control of the tuning button of our radio sets and can tune into a frequency of our choice—the choice between the free spirit and the programmed mind. But this can only happen when we act out of awareness and delink ourselves from the programming we have grown up with.

> As long as we operate from the dimension of the programmed mind, where is the question of exercising one's free will?

However, when we operate from the true self, we break free from the clutches of all the limiting and negative thoughts we have implanted in the mind and to which we get bound. Choices are now made with the awareness of a universal energy or a superior intelligence guiding us right through our journey. Only now is free will in operation, because we have made a deliberate choice to change our programming. When we connect with the true self, we are connected to inner wisdom and are no longer governed by conditioned responses. Now, whatever outcomes that occur are no longer a source of worry. We are assured that, because inner wisdom is the guide, whatever unfolds, even if it is not what we desired, it will be best for us. We are no longer being tossed around in the tidal waves of our inherited karmic tendencies or caught in the snare of our mental programming. There is no dissonance in our minds about expecting things to be some other way.

Sri Ramakrishna Paramhansa says that as one progresses on the spiritual journey, the rope of freedom could become longer, allowing for greater access to free will. Life guided by operation of the free will does not have to follow a preordained pattern, because we can make a deconditioned choice in terms of how we wish to experience our life. In this sense we can take charge of our destiny to follow.

What shifts can we bring about in our thoughts to make peace with our circumstances?

Once we accept that our choice of thoughts make or break the level of peace we can have, then no matter how disturbing our circumstances may appear, by an appropriate shift in thoughts, our life condition can be altered. Let's take a look at how different streams of thoughts can be shifted to make a positive difference to our lives.

- **Wanting certainty *vs* embracing uncertainty and being comfortable with it**

Will my marriage be a successful one? Will my children get admissions into their educational institution of choice? What if a recession comes around and I lose my job? What if natural calamities take place? What if an accident occurs involving me or my near and dear ones?

These are typical questions we may have grappled with some time or the other. Living with uncertainty is often not comfortable for many of us because it requires us to contend with fear, anxiety and worry about how our life will play out sometime in the future.

> The problem is that the mind has been programmed to relate only to that which it believes to be 'known'. And that which is in the realm of unknown, the mind is wary of.

The truth is, everything in life is uncertain. That's the way it always was and that's the way it always will be. There are a multitude of factors that can positively or adversely affect our future. Thus, there will undeniably be situations in life that are well beyond our control. A farmer could slog the whole day ploughing his field, adding manure and doing whatever it takes to ensure a good harvest, but his efforts may not bear fruit if the monsoon fails. This would suggest that there will always be some factors in operation that are beyond our control, and hence outcomes may not always materialise, despite our best efforts.

So why then do we hanker after sureties? When we do so, our energies are never focused on the moment, but are frittered away in needless worries and fears. And not living in the now means we become prisoners of our imagination, depriving ourselves of aliveness and the potential of creating something of value.

Moreover, even if everything in life was certain and we knew exactly how our life would shape up, wouldn't that become very insipid, stale and boring? Where would be the possibility of experiencing the freshness and adventure that life can present us with? Where would be the scope for endless possibilities that we could encounter for our growth and that the mind may not have even conceived? So wouldn't it make more sense to become comfortable with the idea of living with uncertainty and gracefully embracing it? Why not live out our heart's true desires and trust that whatever outcomes unfold in the future would be exactly the ones that are intended for us?

- **Resisting situations *vs* acceptance of each moment as it is**

There is a universal law: 'What you resist will only persist'. So why resist 'undesirable' situations that arise? Why not accept them as they are? Whenever we are confronted with unfavourable circumstances, it is very natural for us to complain and ask: 'Why did this have to happen to me? What did I do to deserve such unpleasant outcomes and experiences?'

> When things went in your favour and you experienced joyful circumstances, at those times did you ever ask: why me? Is it fair then to question events that are supposedly not working in your favour?

When things don't go our way, the inner resistance works to 'push' away the problem because we can't cope. But resisting only saps us of our energy. Instead of it being channelised towards finding solutions, which always exist, it gets depleted through its constant preoccupation with the situation.

> You would notice that it's only in the mind where resistance is being produced to all that is happening on the outside.

But where is the resistance in the universe? Nowhere. And since we and the universe are interconnected, then by resisting are we not going against the flow and natural rhythm of the universe? Much of our tensions stem from our resistance to circumstances that are not 'agreeable' to us.

Moreover, what is the sense in resisting something that has no permanence? Situations come and go—whether positive or negative. These happen in accordance with natural laws. In fact when you look at life closely, isn't everything just transient and fleeting? So why not just let things pass?

> The only litmus test for us is whether our actions are based in awareness and in tune with our free spirit, rather than performed through impulses driven by the conditioned mind.

Emotional detachment from what is happening around us prevents the need to take a judgement call and label anything as good or bad.

The universe has its own mechanism and things will happen the way they are meant to, not with our permission and not always according to the way we want them to unfold. It's we who may not be in sync with its rhythm and if so, it's time to reflect.

> So, if and when you experience a low life condition or you are feeling stuck and bogged down, just check what your mind may be resisting and struggling with.

You might argue that 'accepting things as they are' is tantamount to having an excuse for inaction. It is not to suggest that we do not have a responsibility to act. Recognising that, along with the divine powers, we are the co-creators of our circumstances, we must take the responsibility to act wherever appropriate.

- **Trying to control life *vs* 'letting go' and being in alignment with its natural flow**

It is common for most of us to frequently ask ourselves: 'Why isn't life going *my* way?' or 'Why can't life just give to me whatever I want?'

In a sense we seem to demand a 'remote control' in our hands with which we can direct life in the direction of our desires. We grow forlorn and disillusioned because what we wish for does not materialise, or it does not happen in the time frame of our liking.

When the intention of what we wish to create arises within us, an expectation sets in and we grow impatient to experience a changed set of circumstances. Our internal struggle starts and our level of discomfort increases. Caught in the grip of our personal struggle:

- We are unable to place our faith in the workings of the universe. In a sense, our voice to the universe is: 'Oh, looks like this is not going to happen'.

  These self-defeating thought vibrations are picked up by the universe just like the antenna of a mobile. The universe, non-judgementally, simply reflects back the message conveyed like an echo. So whatever we wanted to create cannot be experienced because our voice to the universe was one of self-denial.

- We try to 'pull' outcomes our way. We are not giving the laws of the universe a chance to operate in their natural way. By doing this, we are trying to interfere with natural processes and thus we put nature in a position to create an opposing force, which will resist what we are trying to obtain. Thus, we wonder why things are not working in our favour, leading to further despair.

When you see the entire workings of the universe, you might agree that these are governed by laws and phenomena, many of which are perhaps beyond the comprehension of human intelligence. Surely there must be a higher intelligence at work that keeps all our vital organs working, even when we are not in a totally conscious state of sleep. Or makes a caterpillar change its form to a butterfly and a seed transform into a tree. The beauty of life is in seeing the tree grow, with the unfolding of its branches, leaves, flowers and fruits—all the grand workings of existence. Any interference by us in the process of nature, such as trying to force open a bud, would only end up in destroying what would turn out to be a lovely flower—a beautiful creation of the universe.

We have no clue as to how a seed eventually transforms into a fully grown tree. Divine energy, however, knows it, and just works according to its infinite intelligence and its timeline.

There is a certain order in all workings, and not for a moment do we doubt whether the functions of creation will be diligently performed. In that sense we are trusting of the universe and the unfolding of its various phenomena. In this respect, we are non-interfering in the way the universe continually expresses itself.

Why then do we interfere with the universe when it comes to manifesting our desires? Why not instead just 'release' our intention to the divine intelligence, which will then work to co-create the experience that will be in our best interests?

> The key check point for us is only: Are we trusting of the universe, 'allowing' its superior intelligence to work on our intention, taking necessary action whilst being open, receptive and available to receive its blessings?

The truth therefore is that it is futile to struggle against the forces of life, nature and its rhythm. Trying to gain desired outcomes through controlling life is trying to do the impossible.

We often think the only way to create happiness is to try to control the outer circumstances of our lives, to try to fix what seems wrong or to get rid of everything that bothers us.

But the real problem lies in our reaction to those circumstances. What we have to change is the mind and the way it experiences reality. The only thing we can control is ourselves, by reprogramming the mind with value-creating, empowering thoughts.

> Yesterday I was clever, so I wanted to change the world. Today I am wise, so I am changing myself.
>
> —Rumi
>
> *Sufi mystic and poet*

If you were to see a flowing stream of water you would have observed its special character. There is a certain vitality in the flow. To keep flowing is the very nature of the stream. There is a sense of detached harmony and melody in its flow. It remains unperturbed by the scores of rocks and boulders it might encounter during its course. Instead of stopping its flow, it merely rides over them and continues unabated. In doing so it simply and gracefully accepts their existence, passes no judgement on them, does not get into a struggle with them, and just carries on with its karmic and natural flow.

Is there a lesson for us here? The boulders, rocks and other such obstacles represent the problems we all will inevitably face in our lives. What we need to do is to accept these with a sense of awareness and non-judgement, in the realisation that we have the inherent capacity (just like the flowing water) to ride over these obstacles.

Going with the flow would put us in harmonious rhythm with life itself. Then there is nothing to struggle against, or doubt, fear, or worry. There is only a 'letting go' that is required.

> 'Letting go' would mean relinquishing our need to control life and outcomes, releasing all the bitterness, hurt, grudges and unworthy junk we have held on to. It means no fight, no struggle with what is, but relaxing in harmony with the flow of life.

It's about not trying to force outcomes but allowing things to happen and having faith in what will be. The less we anticipate the future, the less disappointment there will be when things do not go as per our wishes.

It's about accepting people and situations in the now, as they are.

It's about aligning ourselves with the larger game plan of nature.

It's about the realisation that the only thing under our control is the attitude and response we bring to situations and circumstances.

Try 'letting go' for a change instead of 'holding on' and see the difference it makes to your life. Does 'holding on' keep you uptight, on a short fuse, in a state of unease and turbulence? On the other hand, if you say to yourself, 'Let it be,' to whatever events happen, with total acceptance and without the need to judge, you may find yourself feeling unburdened, freer and at peace with yourself.

Problems: Should we view them as 'problems' or as springboards and opportunities for our growth?

In your day-to-day life, you experience feelings and emotions that vary from happy to sad depending on how you have interpreted and perceived a specific situation. Any problematic situation or circumstance that causes discomfort, stress and unease is only a cue that something needs to change within us. But all our energies are consumed in trying to change the situation or circumstance as if the situation was the root cause of our troubled state of mind.

What if we change our outlook and view problems from a totally different perspective? Can we choose to see 'hidden benefits' in all events we encounter? That's not to suggest that we are being unrealistic and 'denying' the experience we are going through. It's just that we need *not* be compelled by our thoughts and emotions arising out of the experience.

> We could always change tack and take a position that 'nothing is happening to us' and that 'everything is happening for us' (for our ultimate benefit and growth). We thus make the shift to a value-creating thought: 'What is the lesson here for me?'

No matter what the nature of the problem or crisis we face is, we can always use the situation as the very means (the raw material, so to speak) to process and change our attitude. When we choose to make changes from within, our situation and the circumstances around us change. This is the universal law.

As long as we do not change, we will continue to need the occurrences of such problematic situations in our lives because it is only through such experiences that our growth can happen. The transformation of our lives therefore is not an 'outside job'. It is and will always be an 'inside job'. Because we encounter problems, we can challenge ourselves to rise above them and tap into our inner reservoir to find solutions. In doing so, problems are no longer problems. They become springboards to build a stronger self.

In fact, you may possibly realise later on that, had it not been for the problems you encountered, you may not have become stronger, more compassionate, more confident, more accepting, and more responsible. In fact you now start to see those very problems as a thanksgiving because they have helped you evolve and grow.

> Furthermore, all the so called failures, problems and disappointments we may experience at any given point in time may actually become the cause for our success story in the future.

I recall the case of a very bright candidate who appeared for a final interview with the top management of a large, reputed MNC. The job was a most coveted one, paying very well. For the candidate it would have been a dream come true to work with such a prestigious and renowned organisation. However, the job was not offered to him and the candidate felt shattered at the 'rejection'. He landed a job with another Indian company with a lower salary and lesser responsibility. A couple of years later the fortunes of the MNC company dwindled and pink slips became the order of the day as it embarked on a major downsizing program. Meanwhile the candidate went on to become the CEO of the Indian company with an extremely generous salary, perks and attractive stock options to boast. He was thrilled. From his standpoint now, he must have relished being rejected by the MNC, because were he to have been selected, he may not have actualised his full potential.

So every problem or obstacle we come across is only a mirror reflecting some inherent weakness in us. Each roadblock encountered shows that part of our life that causes us to lose hope and faith.

> The critical issue is how we fundamentally decide to use circumstances in our lives, no matter how traumatic—whether we treat problems and obstacles as an excuse for our failures to perpetuate our weakness, or as catalysts for us to grow and achieve our goals.

Just like an airplane cannot fly without wind resistance, we too cannot grow without problems and obstacles.

You might like to assess for yourselves whether the following empowering thoughts and attitudes could be adopted to cause this change:

- 'I will not let my low life condition and my problematic circumstances consume me, because I am connected to a divine life force that I can tap into for strength and wisdom, and transcend my problem.'
- 'The greater my perceived problem, the greater the potential to overcome it and accomplish my dreams.'
- 'I will choose not to listen to the negative, demoralising and self-defeating voices within me that try to tell me why my situation can't change. When I don't listen to these voices, I make a cause for bringing about a positive transformation in my life. I can then shift my energies from focusing on the problem to finding solutions.'

So why take life so seriously? Why not just relish it moment-to-moment, no matter what the circumstances?

> I don't think Existence wants you to be SERIOUS. I have not seen a serious tree. I have not seen a serious bird. I have not seen a serious sunrise. I have not seen a serious starry night. It seems they are all laughing in their own ways, dancing in their own ways. We may not understand it, but there is a subtle feeling that the whole existence is a celebration.
>
> —Osho
>
> *Indian mystic and spiritual teacher*

Many of us have forgotten what it is to celebrate life. Let's be honest with ourselves. In contemporary times what we are chasing and trying to 'import' from the outside is not real happiness but pleasurable experiences that are all momentary and fleeting. We take recourse to the illusory world represented by fake profiles on social media and 'virtual' entanglements. We get sucked into the quicksand of life's pull and pressures and become a slave to our desires. We get obsessed and fritter away our energies, craving a larger house, more money in the bank, more luxuries, etc. We compare ourselves to others who in our judgement are better 'positioned' in life than we are. In this rat race, we forget what it is to just enjoy all that we have and to just *be with existence*.

We become too serious and ignorant of basic reality, which is:

> Joyful, fulfilling relationships and real happiness can never be brought from the outside. They are contingent on the readjustment of a mental attitude, which frees us from the clutches of the programmed mind. You might discover that a joyful state already exists in the depths of your being but gets shrouded in the unending clouds of the false ego that makes you restless, chasing your wants.

The truth therefore is that happiness exists independent of your circumstances. Whenever you attach preconditions to your happiness or make it contingent upon things happening in the outer world, you won't be able to experience it. This is because when one desire is fulfilled, your mental unrest that attaches your happiness to specific outcomes will show up again in the form of the next craving. You may believe that happiness may arrive one fine day and all will be well. This can never happen.

Happiness can't be reduced to a few desirable experiences. It's only a matter of your choice—choose your thoughts and you can choose to be happy. It would be too naïve to believe that you won't have your moments of sadness. Sure you will. But let's understand that sadness is again a choice you would have exercised because of your thoughts about a given situation and not the situation per se.

So when you alter your mindset and just live in the present moment, you start to live with greater intensity, more purposefully, with heightened awareness. Your living is centred on your being and not on the external trappings of the world. You enjoy doing whatever you are doing because it's coming from the deepest recesses of your inner being—your soul. Life becomes a celebration for you in the true sense.

> I want to sing like the birds sing, not worrying about who hears or what they think.
>
> —Rumi
>
> *Sufi mystic and poet*

And what better way to be happy than to return to our child like self when we needed no specific reason to be happy?

∞

4

YOUR RELATIONSHIP WITH YOUR PARTNER

> Love was always meant to be free-flowing. That's its very nature. Why then do we still expect and demand to possess it?

> Your partner is a spiritual being. Not an instrument to be used and manipulated to fulfil your personal needs for security, possessiveness and self-gratification.

The myth and reality about love

'Love' must perhaps be the most overused, misconstrued and loosely used word we are familiar with.

Expressions such as 'I fell in love', 'It was love at first sight', 'I just love so-and-so (cricketer, film star, writer, etc.)' are commonly verbalised. But are we sure that we do not mistakenly construe liking, infatuation, and lust with love?

Isn't it the physical form of a person that we usually find attracting us to them at the first instance? So infatuation is dependent on 'something' in the person our senses pick up. So intense is the feeling for the other person that our world appears ecstatic and we delude ourselves into believing that we have fallen in love. However, not too late into the relationship that seems like eternal bliss, reality strikes and we find that the infatuation has run its course, and are confronted with the usual relationship issues. It is only then we learn that while infatuation may come with a fierce passion, it lacks the maturity and depth for us to comprehend the nuances of a relationship built on genuine love for one another.

On the other hand, liking others may have its roots in our cultural, religious and belief systems that subconsciously affect our attitudes and behaviour towards others. Or we usually like a person because of some commonly held interests or because the person exhibits certain qualities we like about ourselves. At times, we are drawn to others because we instinctively feel that a particular person would be the right 'fit' in terms of meeting some of our unfulfilled needs and desires—be it for greater security, emotional support or intimacy.

So, much as it would appear that the reason for liking someone is because of something in the other person, often the real reason for liking (or even for disliking) someone is based on ourselves; our self-centredness or the 'I' that wants to 'feel better' through someone else. For instance, some people may like to be part of a group which is not intellectually inclined because it is through this group that they could seek for themselves a relatively 'superior' identity.

In love, on the other hand, the focus can never be on the 'I'. Love can flow only when there is selflessness. As long as there is a feeling of 'wanting', the preoccupation and concern is only with oneself, not the other.

Nor can love be a 'hunger' that craves self-gratification, simply because the other person is reduced to an object or a commodity for satisfying one's urges. That would be sheer lust. And that is humiliation for the person being 'used'.

Liking someone is also often mistaken for love. But isn't there a difference between 'I like you' and 'I love you'?

When you like someone, you do so *because* you find certain traits in the person that are appealing to you. Your focus is not on the total being of that person but only the attributes. And it is on account of these attributes that you may feel comfortable being in the person's company while even having a sense of admiration and respect for the person. Liking is more likely to be superficial, transient and devoid of any commitment or responsibility. However, when you love someone, you don't do so because of anything. No reason is needed. You just give of yourself to the person unconditionally and in total acceptance. Your focus is not on any selective attributes of the person but on the totality of the person's being. You connect with the soul of the person. In love, you just let the other be as is, for their sake, without expecting him or her to change for you. The concern is totally for the other backed with total commitment. Thus, whilst there could be an element of ego at play when you like someone, there is dissolution of the ego in love.

Often, we convince ourselves we are doing service to others because we love them—in reality we might be doing so because it is expected by society, massages our egos, or is our duty. However, duty can often become a 'burden', a kind of an imposition. Love, however, can never be a burden.

Many people go through life believing: 'When I find somebody who loves me, I will feel complete, no longer lonely, and totally secure'. A man who thinks he loves a particular woman may actually be misled into believing that the fulfilment of his own needs and urges is an expression of love. A woman who finds the vacuum of her loneliness filled by the presence and attention of a man in her life may also misinterpret this emotional need and satisfaction thereof for love.

However, a belief in such a 'reciprocal arrangement' is misplaced, because if you want someone to fill a void of emotional, mental and physical emptiness, you have nothing to give to the relationship, for your focus is only on 'taking' or 'extracting'. Sooner or later a sense of dependency is created and this can only lead to resentment by the other person. Dependency gets falsely camouflaged as love since the relationship is governed largely by mutual fulfilment of personal agendas and selfish requirements.

When you choose to be dependent on your partner for all your needs, you unconsciously give the control of your thoughts, feelings, and emotions—in fact your total state of mind—to him or her. Your mental freedom becomes subservient to your partner's sense of domination and manipulation. You start felling chained. Such a kind of dependency that one believes to be love can never be empowering and will only end up being short-lived whilst causing lots of pain and anguish.

In love, you don't experience any 'emptiness'. Your inner being already holds the emotion. It is just waiting to flow and be shared. It is through this sharing with one another that the blossoming of love takes place, and gives meaning to our lives. In love, the focus is not on one's personal needs but on the fulfilment of the other person, on the growth of the other person. Love is not about 'what can I get out of the other?' but 'what can I give to the other?' Real love is freedom. It does not restrict. It does not create dependency. It does not want to take ownership of or possess the other.

A point for reflection:

> If love is indeed an inner treasure, why do we still search for it in others? It would appear that there is a huge demand–supply gap when it comes to love. But why run after something that we carry within us?

Love is sublime. It needs no reason. It is selfless. It just accepts the other person as the person is, not subjecting him or her to a scrutiny of sorts and then deciding whether or not the person is worth loving. Love gives unconditionally of oneself without expectations and doesn't have to be sought.

> Your task is not to seek for love, but merely to seek and find all the barriers within yourself that you have built against it.
>
> —Rumi
>
> *Sufi mystic and poet*

If we think about it, when we erect barriers that obstruct the flow of love from our inner being, it is the same barriers that will not let love flow into us from the external world.

Many would argue that it would be impractical not to have expectations from others—after all, a relationship can never be one-sided. However, love does not measure and keep a tally of what is given and how much is received in return. That would be a commercial contract or a business deal, isn't it? And this is not the nature of love. Does this sound too idealistic? Not quite, because in the grand design of nature it was intended that there be an unconditional relationship between all elements of existence. Just observe the trees. They give us not just their shade, shelter, and fruits, but also the vital oxygen necessary for our survival. Now without nurturing any expectations, the trees naturally receive from us the carbon dioxide which they need for their sustenance. Such is the beauty of this symbiotic relationship of giving and receiving in the natural scheme of things—no demanding, no holding back, but just giving freely. It is worth paying attention to such things.

If you are seeking a partner in your life, it might be worth asking: 'Am I ready for a relationship and marriage? What is my honest reason for venturing into it?'

As you enter into a relationship, it may be worthwhile asking yourself whether you have firstly started to accept and love yourself as you are. Secondly, ask yourself: 'What is my greatest need to be in the relationship?' A candid answer will make things a lot better not only for yourself but for your partner as well.

When you are not comfortable with yourself and are self-critical, not having accepted your imperfections, you transfer the same mindset into the relationship with your partner, resulting in friction and undermining of the relationship. Furthermore, when one is single, it is customary to be tormented by pangs of loneliness and feel something is missing in one's life. So there is a compelling need to draw another person into our life to fill up an emotional vacuum. This invariably becomes the driving force that makes us rush into a relationship in the belief that all will be blissful. Or we get into marriage because we are deeply conditioned into believing that it is a necessity and it is only expected of us to get married.

If this be the case, would not this be a recipe for inviting a sense of disillusionment? For you have unconsciously subcontracted your happiness to your partner with an expectation that he or she is supposed to provide you the emotional nourishment you are hungry for. In a sense you end up 'using' your partner as a means to fulfil your own need. Will this not be a frustrating experience for the one being used?

So it cannot be that a partner will come into your life to 'complete' you and bring along a platter full of ingredients for your happiness, security and well-being. You may not be as 'lonely' as you were earlier but now you could bogged down by arguments, bickering, unrealistic expectations and burdens of responsibilities and duties.

That's why it's so important to ask yourself the real reason for venturing into marriage. Of course you might readily say: For companionship, physical intimacy and to raise a family. Sure, at one level this makes sense. But if this was just the case, why do so many marriages end up being unsuccessful? So there is more to it than we may believe. Let's think about this:

Is it not because you first feel adequate, worthy, complete by yourself and self-assured that you can meet your potential partner with an open mindset and positive qualities?

Is it not because you already have love residing within you that you feel the need for love to find an expression and that's why you seek a partner with whom to share this love with? After all, love is not a static but a dynamic energy. It makes sense only when it is allowed to flow freely.

Is it not because you respect your partner as a unique individual with their own aspirations and callings that you feel you can contribute towards their growth?

Once you are convinced about your honest reason for venturing into marriage, you may wish to guard against rushing into a relationship. Relationships need patience and it is vital that partners feel comfortable with themselves before they start feeling comfortable with one another.

> Don't rush into any kind of relationship. Work on yourself, feel yourself, experience yourself. Do this first and you will soon attract that special loving other.
>
> —Russ Von Hoelscher
>
> *Author*

And if by chance you have been divorced and wish to have another go at a relationship, you must check with yourself: 'Am I just seeking another person in my life on the rebound?' For if your honest answer is yes, you are only looking at serving your self-fulfilling need for avoiding your loneliness and shoring up your lowered self-worth from your previous experience; the 'new' person in your life was just an instrument in the process. Unless you feel that one broken relationship does not define you, that you have learnt some lessons from your past experience and that you have no dearth of love to share, you are unlikely to experience a healthy relationship going ahead.

> Many people are mistakenly led to believe that moving from one relationship to the next one would be a solution to their problem, that things would now be hunky-dory. However, it comes as an uncomfortable surprise when they find that the problems that they had in the previous relationship also move along with them.

The dynamics of a marriage

Marriage—is it increasingly getting subjugated to a personal and social convenience? Is it something people get into because of a 'you scratch my back, I scratch yours' syndrome—a kind of a convenient arrangement where mutual satisfaction of needs becomes the primary driving force? Or because of an unspoken and unwritten 'contract' that keeps each other away from pangs of loneliness and insecurity? Or because society equates having a loving relationship between two partners only with marriage, validated by law and religious institutions?

> But can a relationship based on a fixed institution, social and personal conveniences truly stand the test of time?

Relationships between couples in many instances follow a typical and predictable pattern characterised by:

Getting swept off their feet, looking into each other's eyes with dreams of spending great times together, promising to each other that their love will be eternal, and venturing into all the rituals of marriage before embarking on a honeymoon with visions of rapturous moments of intimacy. So far so good.

But not too long into the marriage, when the couple start to live under one roof and the veils and masks (which have been protectively guarded so far) begin to drop off, the tribulations start. Over time, the couple begin to find a mental, emotional and physical 'distance' between them setting in, leaving them wondering what happened to the eternal nature of that love, which now seems more a dream than reality. Further, they wonder how 'Mr/Ms Right', who appeared 'right' earlier on doesn't seem so 'right' now.

Yes, it's a fact. Couples are divorcing a lot faster today. According to a recent report (*Hindustan Times* report, 2015), the divorce rate in India has increased 13 times in the last 10 years.

These statistics do not necessarily suggest that couples had more harmonious relationships earlier on than in present times. There were many factors which dissuaded people from ending their marriages if they were unhappy in the relationship. Expectations by a conditioned society, which considered it a taboo for people, especially women, to divorce, economic dependence of women on their husbands, and the stigma attached to single women were some key factors. However, with more women becoming economically independent, changing societal mores and couples opening up to the fact that they are not answerable to society for what is a question concerning their lives, more couples are willing than before to have their marriages annulled.

It would also appear that, of those partners who do not separate legally, quite a few experience little pulsating energy in the relationship triggered largely by differing expectations, goals, and opinions.

So what's going on here? Why does being together become burdensome? Why do many couples experience unfulfilling relationships?

Here are some thoughts on the matter for reflection:

- Clearly the purpose of marriage is not to stifle you or bind you. It requires giving space for each other to grow. But growth needs freedom and we become oblivious to the fact that without freedom, love cannot blossom.

> So love and freedom must go hand in hand.
> You cannot divorce one from the other.

But how many couples are truly and readily willing to give freedom to the other—freedom to develop their respective potential, freedom to make mistakes, freedom to find their own purpose, fulfil their dreams and aspirations, and so on? If one is honest, one will find that instead of giving freedom, couples are more inclined towards imposing on their partners strictures and restrictions, drawing barriers and not giving the other sufficient space. When you do not give freedom, you severely compromise the relationship because implicit in freedom is the virtue of being trusting, and when there is no trust there can be no relationship and no love. The universal and natural laws are such that love can just not flourish unless it operates in a 'free' environment. No wonder that with the curbing of freedom, love just vanishes and the marriage is on the rocks.

- As couples evolve in their marriage journey, is it not common to find themselves being taken for granted. In quite a few instances, there develops a need to control and dominate the partner by imposing themselves and their views on them, there are expectations galore, often boredom sets in on account of routines that become mundane, and communication between them starts to recede. The relationship becomes akin to a robot performing its tasks mechanically, bereft of feelings of affection and respect. Even sexual intimacy gets reduced to an 'act' performed for satiating respective carnal desires. Not surprising, then, that lives of these couples get riddled with constant strife and the partners begin to feel trapped, suffocated and bound in the relationship. When this happens, the beauty of the relationship gets lost.
- Partners in a marriage or even in a relationship struggle at a personal level because they often try to fit the other

person into a framework of expectations. Would this not be unreasonable, since it's a fact that no two people can ever be at the same level of understanding and each comes with their own set of unique beliefs, experiences and exposures? And when you harbour expectations that are resisted, will you not invite disappointment, hurt, anger and disillusionment? You get married to share love with your partner but if you don't let your partner be themselves and only keep twisting them to fit your own image, it's time to contemplate and ask yourself:

> Are you truly in love with your partner or are you in love with your ego and the reflection of yourself you wish to see in them?

On the other hand, once both partners start focusing on what value they can bring to the relationship rather than what they can get out of the relationship, there is no question of holding expectations that will remain unfulfilled, leading to the souring of a relationship. So, would not enjoying giving and receiving love, growing whilst contributing to the growth of the partner, sharing moments of joy together whilst supporting each other during difficult times, be the vital glue that keeps the relationship robust and lasting?

- The concept of a 'perfect' marriage is a myth, since there is no 'perfection' in the partners coming together. As such there will be grounds for differences, at times leading to animated arguments and fights. Sure enough, this is a phenomenon to be expected. Both partners have their share of positive qualities along with their respective imperfections and flaws. *The point is: On what are the partners focusing?* When you are operating from the ego, there is a tendency to focus on the flaws in the other, on what's 'missing' in them, and to disparage them. However, if you truly love your partner, you love them as a whole, regardless of their flaws, and you even learn to cherish their uniqueness.

- In quite some marriages, there is a sense of frustration and helplessness that sets in because one or both partners can't seem to 'control' or 'change' the other. Perhaps they are deluded into believing that by controlling or changing the other to conform to certain codes of thought and behaviour, they will be happy. The truth is that whilst one partner may get control, the other partner will only feel bitter and resentful. It would only lead to anguish and heartburn. So where is the space left for harmony in the marriage?

> But we can always choose to relinquish our need to control and to change our partner by operating from the dimension of love, rather than from the ego. Only by focusing on changing and controlling ourselves can we create room and an environment for positive and healthy changes to occur in the relationship.

So what would it take for marriage, love and freedom to blissfully coexist?

At first instance, the harmonious coexistence of marriage, love and freedom may sound like a very tall order. In reality though, as much as it may appear difficult, it's not impossible. Here are some thoughts for mulling over that may hold some promise for marriage to blossom and grow with love and freedom at the helm. See if they resonate with you.

- A marriage by itself has no meaning till both partners put into it what they already hold inside themselves, which is an abundance of love. When you give your love freely to your partner without holding back and *not demanding* it, you may invariably find love coming back to you. Why let love be used as a bargaining mechanism that makes the giving of love conditional upon receiving it. The path to a happy marriage is through the heart and not the mind. Since the conditioned mind is driven by the ego, it will only erect walls of 'separateness', whereas marriage can truly work only when love is allowed to flow freely in a spirit of 'oneness' between the couples.
- When you get married, no doubt you become united in togetherness, but if love and freedom have to flow freely through the relationship, it will call for treating each other not as objects or possessions but as spiritual beings who have come together to experience joyful togetherness through give and take. Loving your partner can never be a process of possessing them, because wanting to possess is only an egotistical drive that will end up suffocating the relationship.
- In a marriage, communication plays the vital role of understanding each other and growing together. For this it's important that a space be created by the partners so that they can talk to each other candidly, freely, and without fear.

> Allowing each other to express their innermost feelings sans any inhibitions and without the tendency to be judgemental paves the way to building a robust relationship.

In fact, there is no loss of face or shame in letting our most vulnerable selves be known to our partner. Admitting our faults, mistakes and shortcomings to our partner may often be difficult because of the compulsions driven by the ego, but if done, can only serve to bring our partners closer and strengthen the trust between us.

At times, even if partners share moments of silence in serene togetherness, there is an invisible communication that is at work, conveying intangible messages of the love and beauty of the moment.

- In many marriages there will be times of deep conflicts arising out of a host of factors. Many of these would, in reality, be quite superficial but the 'minor' differences often degenerate into a serious and hostile environment, threatening the very foundation of the marriage. At times we could be impulsively drawn into considerations of divorce. When this happens, let's understand that it's not a war being waged where someone has to emerge as a victor. It's a signal from the universe that there is something that needs to change within the partners. An opportunity is being created for growth to happen.

> For souls in growth, great quarrels are great emancipators.
>
> —Logan Pearsall Smith
>
> *American-born British essayist and critic*

Often when we are angry or irritated with our partners, are we not exposing an unresolved and unhealed aspect of ourselves? There is something *within* us that gets kindled, which just refuses to accept what our partner has said or done. So we choose to hold on to the hurt, disappointment or the pain within us. But isn't that *our own* doing? What if we chose not to let anything our partner said or did get 'pasted' on to us and allowed it to just 'drop' off?

Once we become aware of this and make our connection with the true self, we create an opportunity for self-healing. Furthermore, by recognising that our partner is not defined by any exhibition of lower-order traits, if they show up, but that he/she has the potential to transform these into higher order traits at any moment (anger can be transformed into compassion, greed can be transformed into contentment, and so on), we remove the barriers that come in the way of freely loving the other.

- No marriage became great because couples without any blemishes come together to tie the knot. Let's face it—there are no perfect couples out there. After all, each partner in a marriage relationship will come as a composite package and not tailored or customised to meet each other's desired specifications. Expecting partners to be perfectly compatible with each other would be a pipe dream.

> What counts in making a happy marriage is not so much how compatible you are, but how you deal with incompatibility.
>
> —Leo Tolstoy
>
> *Russian author, essayist and philosopher*

Marriage becomes a truly fulfilling experience when couples, despite their respective inadequacies, choose to accept, respect and in fact enjoy one another's differences and idiosyncrasies. Why should we not accept our partner's flaws and imperfections? After all, don't we ourselves have them, too?

But such acceptance does not come easily. In fact, it is an inner struggle simply because you go into a relationship with expectations, with thoughts of: 'I want the person to be in a way that appeals to me'. You carry some fixed and inflexible notions about the kind of mould your partner should fit into. You are happy if this happens, disappointed if it does not. But once you accept your partner as he/she is, just as you may be accepted for who you are, you need not struggle with yourself in terms of wanting your partner to be 'different'. Acceptance of your partner does not mean that you are making a big compromise or an uncomfortable sacrifice. It means that you have gracefully unburdened yourself of the expectation that your partner needs to unnecessarily change in a manner that is suited to you.

- In today's hectic times, it has become so easy to get carried away by our preoccupation with all the external trappings of the digital world, comprising of our laptops and mobiles, that relationships with our partners may take a back seat. Only when there is contentment and harmony at home can you find all other activities and pursuits to be meaningful and enjoyable. So why should not a relationship with your partner be your first priority?

- In many marriages it is also found that after children arrive, partners tend to somewhat neglect each other. Surely children will be the focus of most of the parents' love and attention, but since love needs to be regularly nourished between partners, why should it be rationed once they have had children?

A sustainable, fulfilling marriage cannot happen on its own. It calls for a commitment and investment from both partners to experience joyful togetherness. Both partners are ever changing and evolving in their journey of a shared life. What matters is whether they make a resolve backed by sincere efforts not to allow any 'distance' to set in.

> In marriage, each partner is to be an encourager rather than a critic, a forgiver rather than a collector of hurts, an enabler rather than a reformer.
>
> —Dr H. Norman Wright
>
> *Author and licensed marriage, family and child therapist*

At any point in time, partners have a choice:

> To operate from love, which is about giving yourself fully and joyfully to your partner, or to operate from a need-based, self-centred, egocentric dimension, which will only tend to alienate your partner.

If you can see in your partner a true friend, someone who is not an extension of yourself but who possesses a 'core' and innate uniqueness you respect, chances are you have already laid the foundation for what could be a thriving married life. So, whilst every good friend may not necessarily be a great marriage partner, a prerequisite for a fulfilling marriage should be a partner who you have been able to cultivate great friendship with—someone who brings a smile to your heart.

∞

5

YOUR RELATIONSHIP WITH FAMILY, FRIENDS AND SOCIETY

"In the ultimate scheme of things, every relationship, whether with family, friends or society, is not just about engaging with each other. It's about growing while contributing to the growth of others we have a connection with.

"Let us not look for ourselves in those whom we have a relationship with.
That would be the ego at work. The ego and genuine relationships based on love and respect shall always be mutually exclusive.

We all need healthy relationships for our well-being. Why do they matter so much?

The relationships we experience with people who come in contact with us have a deep bearing on our well-being—physical, mental, emotional and even spiritual. At the core of relationships are the emotional bonds and ties that serve each and every individual's primary need to remain connected with one another. In the long run, wealth and possessions accumulated fail to give one any 'inner' comfort if relationships have not been endearing. Let's accept this: Life seems shallow and insipid in the total absence of healthy relationships.

> Relationships are more important than Life, but it is important for those relationships to have Life in them.
>
> —Swami Vivekananda
>
> *Spiritual leader and founder, Ramakrishna Mission*

It is generally observed that people who have harmonious relationships through loving family ties, sincere and genuine friends (even if they are just a few), friendly neighbours and supportive colleagues at the work place, are better positioned to withstand life's challenging and stressful situations.

Through meaningful and fulfilling relationships, one can be in a positive frame of mind and ward off periodic feelings of despair and depression. Having a support system, which one can always go to for freely sharing one's concerns, anxieties and worries, goes a long way in releasing debilitating, bottled-up emotions. With such well-wishers around, the gravity of the perceived problem is diminished and the attention gets redirected to looking at solutions, which the otherwise tormented mind may not be able to conceive on its own.

Relationships are also a great channel for our learning and growth. People who come in contact with us are like mirrors reflecting to us certain aspects and tendencies about ourselves that the programmed mind may not be aware of. Often these tendencies represent the barriers we need to overcome in order to have fulfilling relationships, firstly with our own selves and then with others. However, we are so conditioned and obsessed with passing judgements on all those we encounter in our lives that we remain unaware that every interaction, and the manner in which we respond and engage with people, actually hold some lessons for us. Once we become aware of this, we begin to appreciate that people are actually the medium brought to us by the universe through which we continue to grow in our journey whilst also being mirrors to others for their own evolutionary growth.

Finally, come to think of it, when one is in the twilight years of life and realises that it may soon be time to leave the world, what will matter is not how much wealth one accumulated, how much fame and adulation one received, or the status one rose to. What will matter is only whether you have your near and dear ones with you in those last moments. That's when realisation sets in that relationships are all that matter in life.

Relationships within the family—with parents, children, and in-laws. Can we not create a harmonious space for all?

One of the biggest challenges for families to remain connected is the hectic schedules we all maintain in today's frenetic pace of life. It may be an irony of sorts that whilst technology has been a great enabler in getting people connected, there may be fewer 'emotional connections' being experienced between members of the family itself. Cut to a typical family situation where each member is deeply 'immersed' in a world of their own, built around their respective laptops and mobiles, and you get the picture. This is not to suggest that there is a wilful 'disengagement' of the family members from one another taking place at a conscious level. However, so programmed and wired to the digital world are we that we could possibly be unmindful of something precious that we could be missing out on—which is experiencing the joys of togetherness, bonding, and those special shared moments that make for a truly fulfilling family life.

Relationship with parents

The relationship you have with your parents is unique in more ways than one. After all, you have a long history being together with them ever since your birth. Having been cocooned in love and affection with a solid support system, constant guidance and hand-holding, you grow up developing the deepest of emotional bonds and ties. But that's not all. The nature of this relationship undergoes changes as you evolve and your parents, too, add years to their lives. It is the changing dynamics of the interactions that make it possibly one of the most challenging and sensitive relationships you have.

Having positive relationships with parents can be a very rewarding and enriching experience. But it's not always easy.

To start with, unless you are inwardly contented as you are and true to yourself, you are unlikely to demonstrate your true love, affection and kindness to them. And this entails taking personal responsibility.

As you reach adolescence and later turn into adults, the years ahead start to pose challenges to the nature of your interactions for a variety of reasons:

- Your parents grew up in a generation wherein their value systems, beliefs, opinions and views about life were influenced by a certain social and cultural environment prevailing in those times.
- With fast-paced development, major technological, economic and cultural changes, you got exposed to an environment with different belief structures, societal norms and attitudes. These resulted in mindsets and behavioural patterns, often contrasting with those of your parents, leading to conflicts with them.
- As a teenager and later on as an adult, your inclination to spend more time outside the family increases with your need to be more independent and assert yourself, getting stronger. This may not be easily accepted by your parents, who are 'programmed' to be protective of you, to give lots of unsolicited advice and to influence your thinking and actions. Sure enough they may be doing this, wanting only the very best for you, but you may end up perceiving their cause to be insensitive, burdensome, imposing and overbearing. You may start to label them as 'interfering' and 'control freaks'. Such a feeling may manifest itself in

the form of irritability and low levels of tolerance whilst interacting with them.

- Once you grow up as adults and start your own families, your level of involvement and time spent with parents tends to go down. This can lead to disillusionment on the part of your parents, who are now ageing and starting to feel bereft and isolated. While they understand and appreciate that you now have your responsibilities towards your acquired family, there is nevertheless a sense of disquiet and a feeling of being neglected if you can't find time for them or communicate with them on a regular basis.

Notwithstanding sensitivities in interactions with your parents as their children, whether teenagers or adults, you always have the choice to build warm and sustainable relationships with them. This itself is a journey and an ongoing process. Once you decide to take personal responsibility for the relationship, you might like to consider the following guiding elements that serve as the bedrock for nurturing loving relationships with your parents. Why do these work? Simply because you shift the focus from the needs of your own ego and its interplay to building connections that find their roots in love, compassion and empathy. Here they are for you to consider:

- **Expressing appreciation and gratitude**

Your parents showered you with their love and went out of their way to bring you up, keeping your best interests in mind. Surely they may have had a role to play in your 'conditioning', but is that something you want to hold against them? After all, they must have been conditioned by their own parents, too. So does not their unselfish intent and motive for wanting the very best for you be deserving of your appreciation and gratitude for them?

Quite often we may get frustrated by what our parents are not doing or can't do for us. In such situations we could always choose to acknowledge and value all the good things they have done and continue to do for our well-being and growth. Taking parents for granted or 'using' them for our selfish purposes may be the last thing we want to do. Thus, demonstrating our appreciation, affection, regard and care with simple gestures and actions could go a long way in nurturing healthy relationships with them.

- **Acceptance of your parents as they are**

Why not gracefully accept the fact that you are different from your parents and it is fine to be so? Realise that your parents are a product of their own unique upbringing and life experiences, and of the social norms and moral and cultural belief structures they were exposed to. Often we ourselves grow up conditioned by our environment, with images and notions of what 'ideal' parents should be. Let us understand that unless we drop our closely held beliefs of ideal parents and the expectations that go with it, we cannot allow the relationship with our parents to blossom.

Also, let's just accept that our parents aren't perfect, just as we are not. Expecting them to be someone else, or even comparing them with parents of your circle of friends, would not only be unreasonable but would not be conducive to building a healthy relationship with them.

- **Having open, free, frank communication**

Lack of an open, free and candid communication is probably the most common problem that leads to strained relationships. Either we hold back from engaging with each other or we do not express our innermost feelings, largely out of a fear in terms of how they would be received or tolerated. Hence, we often choose the safety of maintaining propriety whilst letting issues simmer inside of us. Opening up fearlessly and candidly, however, can let your parents know exactly how you are feeling and appreciate where you are coming from. The tricky part about open communication, however, is that it could sometimes border on being accusatory—but it doesn't have to be so.

There could undoubtedly be times when you do not agree with your parents, be it their value systems, beliefs, ideas of right and wrong, or their very parenting style. So be it. That would not justify any exhibition of hostility towards them or not being courteous and affectionate. You can, regardless, continue to show your reverence to them by first being a good listener to their point of view and politely discussing things over by presenting your own perspective. A healthy dialogue without in any way undermining the dignity of your parents will foster a congenial atmosphere within the family.

One could always choose to raise issues and express one's feelings in an honest manner without being hurtful. Whilst not communicating with them well enough is not going to help the relationship, playing the blame game, giving vent to your frustrations and showing disrespect is only going to make matters worse. Instead, being empathising, and communicating in a language of love with a spirit of working through your problems and sorting them out, would invariably work to each other's benefit. Let us also not underestimate the true worth of our parents, their ready willingness and capacity to be our best friends when it comes to understanding and helping resolve the deepest of dilemmas and problems that life throws at us.

- **Maintaining your own individuality**

To respect your own individuality is often mistaken for egotism and arrogance. But such a contention would be flawed. As an adult, it is important to realise that a sense of autonomy and being entitled to one's own choices, perspectives and decisions would in fact be healthy. Navigating life by walking in the shadows of your parents' opinions would deny one the confidence, mettle and belief in one's own capabilities and reservoir of strengths. Sure enough, many decisions that you take without any undue influence from parents may go wrong. So be it. That's the only way you will learn and become wiser with experience. There is thus no harm in politely letting your parents know that you are now capable of taking your own decisions. By all means, use them as a sounding board if you genuinely believe you need some wider perspectives, but let the final decision be yours—it is after all *your* life. You may find that with time, instead of parents feeling sore about you not necessarily following their opinions and viewpoints, they may actually end up respecting the strength of your own conviction and self-belief. And just in case they don't, it's still fine because you are living a life of authenticity, following your heart's true callings, which is what really matters.

- **Taking personal responsibility for the relationship**

Quite often we expect parents to take the lead in cultivating strong relationships with us. We expect them to be more understanding, sensitive and tolerant. But let's ask ourselves the question:

> Why must we wait for our parents to be proactive and to change their manner of engagement with us for the relationship to improve? Can we not take the initiative and make it our personal responsibility to nurture warm ties and bonds with them?

By taking personal responsibility, we recognise that we have the inherent power to influence our relationship with them, even though from their perspective we may still be 'kids'.

Our mission is not to expend our efforts in trying to change our parents. If they need to change, let that be their responsibility and inner calling. Our focus instead should be on changing our own attitudinal and behavioural aspects, which can facilitate better interactions with them.

> This does not mean that we can't establish limits or define our boundaries. It's perfectly fine to do so.

For when boundaries are not set, it means that you have 'allowed' yourself to be manipulated, and in abject surrender, you do things or take decisions that are not in sync with your inner true self. However, when you carry the conviction of honouring *your own* needs, you can speak up for what comes from the core of your being—this is your truth, which you choose not to let anyone compromise.

> What is important is the need to stay true to ourselves, not to find faults in our parents. Rather than expecting them to be better parents, let it be our responsibility to be better children.

- **Finding time to be with them and enjoy the togetherness**

No matter how packed your schedules might be or how busy you may be with your other commitments, finding time to spend with your parents is something you may wish to never compromise. It's so easy to take parents for granted as you involve yourself in life's multifarious activities. But think about this: In your own twilight years, will your biggest regret in life be not having accumulated more wealth? Perhaps not. It may well be not having spent sufficient time with your parents whilst they were still around. Many people get consumed with guilt and the deepest of regrets once their parents have moved on, when they realise they had been too busy running a relentless race in this materialistic world.

If you are living with your parents, you can now and then enjoy activities together, such as going for picnics, dining out, going on vacations, etc. Even if you don't live with your parents, staying in regular touch, visiting them on holidays or inviting them over to spend time with you is your way of showing how much you care for them and how much they mean to you.

Once parents age and retire, that's the time when they need not just emotional support but perhaps even physical support, as ailments start taking their toll. Whilst they may not harbour expectations of you to always be around them, this is the time when your presence, affection and patience will be most needed. Your willingness to support them is not out of a sense of duty, but because of your unflinching love for who they are and for all that they have done for you.

Relationships with children

The nature of the relationship parents have with their children constitutes the most impactful of all relationships because it lays the very foundation of their children's future development. When children feel nurtured and cared for with lots of warmth and gentleness, they instinctively experience their first connection with love, intimacy, trust and security. It is largely through parental interactions that children learn how to communicate, behave, develop skills, express themselves through their emotions and foster social bonds.

Whilst there is no doubt that all parents wish to see their children grow up into happy, confident, responsible and successful adults, the facilitating roles that parents can play towards this goal can be quite demanding. Building and sustaining positive relationships with children is not easy and comes with various challenges. Whilst it may be important to instill certain core values in them, there is often an unconscious tendency to go overboard with the rigours of parental conditioning. Moreover, changing dynamics of the relationship with different stages of a child's growth, rapidly evolving societal mores and increased exposure to media and technology can profoundly impact how children see their world and relate with it.

Every relationship between a parent and their child will be unique in its own way, determined by a number of complex factors and the environmental context thereof. Here are a few thoughts on what it could take to have healthy relationships with children.

- **Giving your attention, participation and time**

Warm and endearing interactions with dedicated time taken to be a part of the children's world (listening, talking, playing, taking interest in what they do, being responsive, etc.) sends out the very positive message to them that they matter a lot to the parents. In contemporary times, however, driven by their own work pressures, social engagements, attending to household chores, or even preoccupation with gizmos and gadgets, parents commonly spend less time with their children. In fact, in many cases it is the domestic help who are called upon to 'look after' the children. In the case of economically challenged households, the sheer compulsions of slogging hard to make ends meet, often by both parents, extracts a heavy toll on their time and energies, giving them little scope to look after the children. It is not surprising, therefore, that with such overwhelming environmental and domestic pressures of daily living imposed on parents, many children tend to get neglected and grow up feeling inadequate and insecure in love.

- **Setting the right example**

It is rightly said that while children may not always be good at listening to what their parents say, they are very adept at imitating them. This has deep implications for the development of the child.

In families where there is a lot of friction, arguments, bad-mouthing or even violence, not only does it 'damage' the psyche of children (instills feelings of fear, hatred, violence and insecurity) but children may also grow up to adopt these modes of behaviour and accept them to be normal. On the other hand, maintaining kind and respectful relationships at home provides a healthy environment for children to emulate and grow up in, reflecting positive and respectful interactions with their world.

Another area parents could be careful about is making promises to their children and then not honouring them—whether it is buying them a gift, taking them on a holiday, attending the scheduled parent–teacher meetings, etc. Children then not only feel 'cheated' and forlorn, but also grow up thinking, 'It's okay to break promises because my dad or mum did it'. Trust, which is the bedrock of relationships, also tends to be undermined.

- **Avoiding over-parenting and overprotection**

While it is natural for parents to be a protective shield for their children, often they go overboard in insulating them from the harsh realities of life and the difficult circumstances they would encounter in their journey. There is a typical rationalisation many parents use to justify over-parenting and overprotection:

'We have experienced a lot of struggles in our lives and hence we would not like our children to experience them'. This 'programmed' belief actually becomes the very barrier for the child to face life with aplomb, because the message we convey to them is that they are incapable of handling difficult and challenging situations by themselves. Such children grow up lacking in self-confidence and get into a perpetual dependency mode, believing that their parents will always be there to solve problematic issues for them.

> It is our job to prepare our children for the road and not prepare the road for our children.
>
> —Dr Wendy Mogel
> *Clinical psychologist*

Being overly protective of children also ends up undermining their natural spontaneity and creativity whilst limiting their freedom to make their own independent choices. Life is an adventure that is meant to be fully experienced. Parents could greatly help the cause of their children by allowing them to stand on their own feet and enrich themselves by learning their own realities of life through a multitude of experiences.

As children grow up and enter their teens, parents may need to consider tweaking the manner in which they relate to their offsprings. Teenagers would want their individuality to be respected, and rightly so. The conditioned approach of 'talking down' to them, which only invites resistance and undermines their self-esteem, may need to be replaced with an approach of 'talking with' them. At this stage, treating them as friends without unduly bombarding them with sermons would not only earn parents their respect but also provide a congenial atmosphere for having purposeful interactions.

> Parents need to fill a child's bucket of self-esteem so high that the rest of the world cannot poke enough holes in it to drain it dry.
>
> —Alvin Price
> *Author*

- **Resisting the impulse to be harshly punitive**

We are all familiar with the common adage handed down to us for years, namely 'spare the rod and spoil the child'. Implicit in this contention is the thought that if a child misbehaves, they need to be reprimanded and disciplined. Perfectly fine.

However, would admonishing a child necessarily imply that you have to spank them and raise your hand against them? Many parents would justify their act of using physical beating as an instrument for the child's own good. But do think about this:

> If you raise your hand against your children, are you really trying to instill a sense of discipline or are you only finding an expression for your inner anger, frustration and helplessness in dealing with them?

Children can only end up feeling humiliated at the physical spanking. Apart from developing a fear complex, the children's subconscious could get embedded with emotional wounds and scars that could later manifest in the form of a rebellious nature. This would be counterproductive for the entire family, for rather than curbing their acts of misbehaviour, children might resort to greater levels of indiscipline and misbehaviour. Moreover, children tend to look up to their parents as icons and role models. So from their standpoint they grow up with a belief that violence is not an aberration but a normal and justifiable act.

Thus, instead of delivering harsh punishments, would it not be more beneficial for parents to deal with misbehaviour in a firm and assertive manner, but respectfully and with empathy? Often children get the message that their parents have not liked their misbehaviour simply by the stern and disapproving look they get from their parents. Threatening children with dire consequences would never serve the purpose of reforming them; but what could work is parents communicating with children openly and guiding them as to why their act of indiscipline and misbehaviour is not in the interest of the their holistic growth and well-being.

- **Allowing children the freedom to make life's key choices**

It is a common phenomenon for parents to play a strong, influencing role in determining the direction that their children's lives should take. This is part of their ingrained programming and whether it's the question of choosing academic disciplines, careers or even a life partner, they exhibit a tendency to assert and impose their will on them. The reality, however, is that conditioning them with *your* belief systems and *your* sense of right and wrong, and enforcing decisions that seem appropriate only from *your* perspective, will only stifle the child's creativity and burden them with unrealistic expectations. It will not allow any space for them to connect with their true callings, their own aspirations and what they most seek from life. The end result is more often than not a disillusioned child who grows up feeling frustrated at not being able to pursue goals aligned to their own dreams.

That's not to suggest that parents have no constructive role to play in the matter of choices being exercised by their children. Parents can play a great facilitating role in helping the child discover their unique talents, interests, abilities and skill sets. Having done so, through their unstinted love, encouragement and support, they can provide the very platform for them to undertake the journey of their children's choice, but *not* choose the journey on behalf of their children.

What parents could also do is to avoid passing unfavourable judgements on choices their children have made, especially when the choice exercised is not in conformity with the parents' own wishes. This would only alienate the child. Accepting the child's contrasting journey of life may often be difficult for parents—that's because they are operating from the ego dimension. However, when they operate from the free spirit and from love, they will respect their child's choice. Furthermore, the children, knowing they have their parents backing, will feel motivated to grow to their fullest potential and strive for excellence in their chosen path, which is what parents would ultimately wish for them.

> Why not then give the child their own freedom to make life's key choices, to explore their own world and experience their own reality?

Relationships with in-laws

Managing relationships with in-laws can be extremely tricky because it is an accepted premise that when couples get married, they also marry the respective families. There is an extended and complex relationship structure with interactions inevitably happening between in-laws.

Various research studies have indicated that the relationship with in-laws plays a vital role in influencing the quality of relationship a married couple will have. Dr Terri Apter, a senior tutor at the University of Cambridge and an expert in writing about family dynamics, spent over 20 years interviewing hundreds of families across the world as part of a research project undertaken for one of her books. According to Dr Apter, whilst 75 % of couples reported having a problem with an in-law, only 15 % of mother-in-law / son-in-law relationships were found to be stressful. More than 60% of women felt that the relationship with their female in-law was strained and caused them unhappiness. There are various factors that complicate relationships with in-laws and bring about different degrees of discord, friction and stressful life conditions. Typically perceived symptomatic issues that could result in strife between in-laws could be:

- Daughters-in-law and sons-in-law perceiving their respective mothers-in-law (and even fathers-in-law) to be dominating, interfering (even though often it may be unintentional), self-opinionated and asserting a 'know-it-all' stance by offering unsolicited advice. There would also be expectations in terms of conforming to ideals and values, fiercely guarded by in-laws, as also to their concepts of religious and cultural norms.

- Mothers-in-law feeling isolated and insecure because they perceive the daughter-in-law to be an 'intruder' in the deep-rooted ties of maternal love she has nurtured with her son.
- Sons-in-law and daughters-in-law feeling caught between contrasting situations—trying to please their respective in-laws or just being themselves and wanting their own space.
- Differing perceptions of both the women in terms of their respective roles and conflicting expectations in the relationship. Whilst the mother-in-law believes that she must continue to be the 'primary' woman in the family, the daughter-in-law expects that the mantle of being the primary woman and 'taking charge' of the family reins must now be passed on to her.
- Jealousies between daughters-in-law and sisters-in-law.
- The tendency in many cases (as research reveals) is for the man to side with his mother when she has a conflict with his wife, leaving the daughter-in-law with a feeling of betrayal.
- If the daughter-in-law has been her father's 'little princess', being over protected, pampered and used to having all her demands met, a difficult situation arises for the son-in-law, who feels sore at not being able to measure up to his father-in-law's standards.

Of course, there would be many other causal factors that cause tensions in the relationships between in-laws.

However, it comes as a revelation from Dr Apter's research that one of the prime reasons for strife, particularly between daughters-in-law and mothers-in-law, has little to do with their actual attitudes. The genesis of problems has more to do with deeply conditioned and programmed female norms and codes of conduct created by patriarchal society, which many women find it difficult to shake off. So powerful is the programming that both mothers-in-law and daughters-in-law are invariably suspicious of each other, and feel mutually threatened and fuelled by a sense of insecurity. The 'new' daughter-in-law who comes to the joint family after marriage wants the husband totally to herself whilst the mother-in-law is not able to reconcile with the fact that her son, whom she has nurtured with so much care and love, would now give her much less attention. This mental tug-of-war causes unrest not just for both the women but for the man as well, since he now feels the pulls and pressures to keep both happy.

One finds that in many such families, this typical scenario is accepted as 'normal' and dismissed with a shrug: 'This is the very nature of such relationships', as if to suggest that the universe had planned for such strained relationships and therefore there is nothing one could do about it. However, holding such a 'helpless' perspective would not be healthy as it could sooner or later result in serious discord and negation of peace within the family.

Actually, come to think about it, it's even ironic that there should be a case for disharmony between the two women in the family. After all, every mother-in-law was once a daughter-in-law and every daughter-in-law may one day be a mother-in-law. So it's not too difficult to see the situation from each other's perspective.

It would thus appear that conflicts between in-laws would almost be inevitable. However, having conflicts does not necessarily mean that the relationship has to be unhealthy and damaging. Here are some thoughts on what mindset changes may be necessary to have better quality of relationships with in-laws:

- Deeply embedded in the conditioned psyche of our society are beliefs that portray in-laws as 'problematic' and 'burdensome'. So in a way, the programming is such that even before one starts a relationship with in-laws, one is already operating from a preconceived sense of 'rivalry'. Deconditioning ourselves of this ingrained belief must then be the first step towards trying to cultivate amicable relationships with in-laws. This would require one to shift away from the ego dimension and operate from a feeling of empathy and compassion.
- If relationships between in-laws are often mired in conflict, it's not because someone out there is a 'villain', but because there are deeper psychological issues that simmer under the surface and need to be understood and empathised with (not always easy, though). After all, each person is operating from their own perspectives. It is this understanding that can help explain the behavioural patterns in terms of how they relate with each other and avoid serious confrontation. For instance, a well-meaning act of helping out the couple

in household chores by the mother-in-law may actually be misconstrued by the daughter-in-law as an intrusion. Or a mother-in-law may feel 'slighted' if the daughter-in-law chooses to do some things her way, which is quite different from the way the mother-in-law has been accustomed to.

- Both the women realise that they are not 'competitors' when it comes to seeking time and attention from the man. Each role (mother–son and husband–wife) can peacefully coexist. They just have to 'allow' this to happen.
- The mother-in-law appreciates that the daughter-in-law has left her family to come into a new home. To this extent, the mother-in-law needs to give space to the couple for their relationship to blossom. After all, when the mother-in-law was a new wife, did she not need her own space with her husband without any emotional interference from her in-laws?
- The daughter-in-law is sensitive to realise that the relationship between a mother and son runs deep and is cocooned in love and affection over years of togetherness. By respecting this, she can shift her orientation to an awareness that relationship with her husband and mother-in-law does not have to be mutually exclusive but can in fact be mutually enriching .
- The man understands that love is meant to be given freely and of which there is no dearth in the depths of his being. So it's not as if there is a 'limited' supply and showering love and attention on any one woman would lead to a 'deficit' for the other.

- Its rightly said that there is a potential 'sinner' and shades of grey in every highly evolved person as much as there is potential saint in every person. So instead of both the women focusing on the 'darker' side of the other, what if they were to consciously 'seek' the inherent goodness in one another and relate from this pedestal? That may still not mean that they do not have their differences, but they will start to accept, appreciate and respect their differences.

This requires one to alter the 'glasses' through which relationships with in-laws are traditionally viewed. One can then move past the anxiety syndrome and the accompanying sense of animosity in-laws have been conditioned to accept as being inevitable. Chances of discord arising between in-laws can be significantly reduced when one let goes of attempts to change each other and instead focuses on establishing unambiguous physical and emotional boundaries that are mutually respected. Just as with one's parents, with in-laws too, it is perfectly normal, healthy and even necessary to define such boundaries at the beginning of a relationship itself. These could be, for instance, on matters related to how children should be brought up, time that would be spent with in-laws, or delineation of household responsibilities.

Building amicable relationships with in-laws may not quite be the easiest thing to do, but for the sake of one's well-being and peace of mind, it is well worth approaching the relationship with patience, understanding and commitment.

> Come to think of it, is it not possible that the stereotyped perspective of an 'in-law' is changed wherein one could cultivate good friendship with each other?

Relationships with friends

It is a fact that as we grow in years and become less dependent on our parents, friends begin to play a very prominent role in our life's journey. It is genuine friends who remain through thick and thin with us whilst increasing our sense of belonging and purpose. It is these friends who we turn to when troubled with challenging and traumatic times. It is in them that we can unhesitatingly confide in about aspects and situations we may not always be comfortable sharing with our families. Friends who accept us as we and are ever there for us truly become a treasure to cherish.

> In prosperity our friends know us, in adversity we know our friends.
>
> —John Churton Collins
> *English writer and literary critic*

Cultivating sound and healthy friendships, however, comes with its own set of challenges, trials and tribulations. They can be times when friends could irritate us or hurt us; tempers could flare up, and we could get embroiled in arguments resulting in misunderstandings and conflicts. Whilst such situations could be labeled as 'undesirable', they may also hold the seed for us to bring greater awareness in terms of how we 'handle' friendships.

Let's look at some of the pitfalls that many a time we could possibly be unmindful of and that may result in strained relationships with friends:

- In making friends, we often tend to be guarded whilst revealing our true selves to them. This is because we are wary whether or not we will be accepted by them. But if we are not going to present our authentic self to them, we are not even giving them a chance to accept us wholly as we are. This vitiates the whole process of a close friendship blossoming.
- Even though we know that each person is unique in their own way and is a product of their own upbringing, experiences and conditioning, there is still a tendency to tweak them to fit our image. In doing so, we may wish to ask ourselves a certain question.

> Are we trying to build a genuine friendship or merely wanting to see our own alter ego in them?

Nurturing sustainable relationships with friends would require us to just let them be themselves, to give them the freedom to think and feel as they wish to. Whenever we try to force something that we think is right upon our friend, we should step back and ask: 'Would I like it or even tolerate it if my friend did the same to me?'

- In the course of our frequent interactions with friends, one of the key barriers to having harmonious relationships is getting into long-drawn-out arguments. This is detrimental to the friendship since an argument never validates one's point. It only ends up showing how desperate one is to prove one's point as right. We cling to our own point of view as if it were the only sacrosanct perspective that represents reality. This, as we have seen, is the workings of the ego. But the true self recognises that a viewpoint is only an opinion—just one of the many ways of looking at the same issue. Moreover, opinions can never have any permanence because they are subject to change depending on the new set of circumstances and experiences one undergoes. So isn't having an argument pointless? And even if we disagree with the point of view held by our friends, why can we not do so amicably? This way we can maintain the respect and dignity of the friendship.

- Being overly judgemental of friends is yet another factor that can come in the way of developing close bonds and ties with them.

> Thus, would it not be true to say that when we judge and label others, we are not defining them but are actually defining ourselves, and in the process it is our own inherent prejudices, biases and preset fixations that are being revealed?

Let's say a friend who has had a rift with you over some issue tells you: 'You are a very insensitive, ill-mannered person'. Now, this is a sweeping, unsubstantiated judgement, only demonstrating the person's own anger and frustration. It leads to nowhere and only aggravates the situation further. Instead, if the same person were to say: 'You know something, I really felt hurt and pained at what you said', it's now just an honest feeling being expressed with no aspersions being cast on you. It creates a space for you to reflect on the appropriateness of what was said and helps assuage the situation in a harmonious manner.

- Many a time nurturing expectations from friends ends up leaving one hurt with a residual feeling of bitterness that one carries when expectations are not met. If some of my friends do not lend me money that I badly need, I am quick to label them as uncaring and insensitive, and begin to doubt the depth and sincerity of the friendship. I conveniently forget all the help they may have given to me in the past, during my difficult times. All my attention is focused on this one occasion wherein I felt badly let down. Isn't it I who needs to reflect on the question of whether I am undermining the beauty of friendship by making it contingent upon my needs being satisfied? Could it not be that I am being insensitive, not appreciating that my friends may have their own compulsions and circumstances for not lending me money, and that I should gracefully accept and respect their decision to do so? When we try to 'pull' the other person into meeting some desired expectations, the natural laws create a resistance to whatever we try to force. It is this resistance that manifests itself in the form of a strained relationship.

> But if we could all start to think and feel in terms of what we are giving to relationships (selfless, unconditional bonding) instead of what we can extract out of relationships (a commercial contract of sorts), wouldn't all of us have better relationships, less turmoil, and more peace within us?

- In times of conflict or disagreements, which can always arise, there is always room for healthy dialogue and an appreciation of each other's point of view. But the reality is that our attention is primarily on thinking of how to retort back without listening to the other's point of view. In such a situation one is reacting rather than responding. There is a subtle difference between the two.

The nature of a reaction is essentially impulsive, aggressive, based on an emotional outburst, and provocative. Therefore, it is degenerative and invariably ends up inviting a hostile reaction from the other as well, leading to a feeling of ill will.

Response, on the other hand, is regenerative in nature as it sets aside emotional entanglement and doesn't intimidate. It provides space for a calm and healthy resolution to the conflict whilst respecting the dignity of the other person and maintaining your own humility.

- In the fast-paced society that we live in today, where we increasingly take recourse to the digital world for acquiring friends, we must step back and ask ourselves: What is our real need? Is it just to have a large circle of friends or is it to cultivate healthy friendship?

> Even if you have just a few friends who are their authentic selves, who replace expectations with acceptance, who don't just ask, 'Is there something I can do for you?' but actually demonstrate so by touching your life in positive ways and are trusting of you, consider yourself blessed to have such friends in your life.

However, let's also accept that we live in an imperfect world. So even if you have invested sincere efforts in cultivating good friendships, the transient nature of everything in this life may cause your friends to part ways with you at some point in time, for reasons best known to them. This does not necessarily mean that you were not a worthy friend to them. Nor do you have to become a victim of their decision to walk out on you or label them as 'ditchers'. All it means is that they came as a medium to contribute a specific role in your life's journey whilst you contributed to theirs. Having done so, their part in your life may be over. So why label them and try and hold on to them? There is a larger, intended value-creating purpose in the interaction. So if you or your friends have to move on, so be it. Why lose sleep over it?

Relationships with society

Our relationships also extend beyond the interactions we have with family and friends to cover society at large, be it our relatives, neighbours, or a host of others who we come into contact with. Such relationships also throw a lot of challenges, for it is not uncommon to find disillusionment in these, despite all good intentions.

You may also agree that at one level modern society's preoccupation with materialism and demanding schedules may be creating a kind of social alienation never experienced before. At another level, even those we do manage to interact with could possibly rub us the wrong way, irritate us, make us resentful and bitter, and keep us on the edge.

> But if we look at things dispassionately, our struggle with such relationships occurs because people do not always behave in ways that we expect them to or do not fulfil their duties as responsible citizens.

We can only exercise our due responsibilities, but why lament if others do not discharge theirs? It is common for us to hold behavioural expectations from society and to judge them by standards defined by us. But how can we become the arbiter of their behaviour? Let us accept that each person in society is a product of their own unique upbringing, sets of experiences, and exposure to a certain environment, and is acting in accord with these. Are we also not acting and behaving on the same premise—a product of our own unique conditioning? So how can we judgementally decide who is right? In our interactions, people are going to bring their own perspectives—that is *their* outlook.

Consequently, all of the irritation, anger, frustration, and impatience comes to the fore because these are residing in us. It's not as if others are transplanting such negative emotions in us. While it is quite in order to allow yourself to feel and express anger when it is warranted, you may want to focus on the issue and how it affects your life condition rather than blaming others.

Thus, the aspect of accepting others without judging them becomes critical for our own peace of mind. However, acceptance should not be misconstrued for weakness on our part in the sense of tolerating aberrations that are detrimental to our and society's interests.

We cannot change how people treat us or what they say about us. All we can do is change how we respond to them. There will also be people who are jealous of us and not our well-wishers. But why hate them or harbour ill-will against them? They must have found something in us of real worth to feel jealous about. That's their problem and their own journey. Why should we build up negative emotions? Let them just be.

However, there could be times when you may find your time frittered away and your energy levels depleted by relationships that are unfulfilling and harmful to your emotional well-being. If so, you may want to ask yourself how you feel about the nature of your relationship—whether it is genuinely exuding love, creating value and contributing to your growth, or is lacking in love, warmth and respect. Or you find yourself being exploited and used, and feel your growth is being stunted.

> If by any chance you feel that a relationship is not healthy and you have not been able to experience an open, genuine and endearing friendship despite all your sincerity, you may need to let it go.

It is, after all, only in the letting go of or disconnection from unhealthy relationships that you can feel free in the true sense of the word.

∞

6

YOUR RELATIONSHIP WITH YOUR WORK AND CAREER

"The kind of work you do does matter a lot—but only to your ego. But when you operate from your true self, what you do has little significance. What matters is whether your heart loves doing whatever it desires. It is this flow of energy that gives meaning to your work and makes for an enriching experience.

"The solutions to the problems of a ruthlessly demanding work environment leading to stress, insecurities and mental turbulence will not come from exercising the mind. They will come from deep within—the spiritual centre, which is a repository of pure wisdom.

The workplace—a great influencer of our state of well-being

We spend a substantial portion, perhaps over a third of our lives, at the workplace, whether pursuing careers in organisations or managing our businesses. As such, our state of overall well-being is significantly influenced by the quality of the relationship we nurture with our work and careers. A joyful working environment and deriving a sense of purposefulness is not just good for our mental and physical health, but also creates a mindset conducive for healthy relationships within the family. On the flip side, dissatisfaction at work, and an unhealthy environment and culture, could vitiate one's peace and inner contentment, whilst also jeopardising what could otherwise be a harmonious family life.

The definition of the most beneficial work to be engaged in can have no universal acceptance, since this has to be assessed in the context of a prevailing social, economic, political and geographical environment. Moreover, it would also be a function of an individual's outlook, personal aspirations, and unique circumstances at any given moment, which could vary with time. However, whatever is the nature of the work we do, it is increasingly becoming important to love what we do. Thankfully in today's times there are many more options, whether in the choice of careers or even entrepreneurship. Moreover, it's no longer all about the paycheck or the financial returns, but also about freedom and flexibility at the workplace. It's also about deriving a sense of meaning and larger purpose, appreciation and recognition for goals achieved, a feeling of having created value, and the opportunity for enhancement in learning, with fulfilment of personal aspirations and growth.

Of course, let's be sure that there are going to be no perfect jobs or businesses out there wherein you can keep ticking off each item in your checklist. Choices would need to be based on relative prioritisation of desired attributes and on listening to the inner voices that reflect your life's true callings.

Increasing challenges at the workplace in contemporary times

It is a well-accepted fact that both the internal and external environments for organisations and the overall business landscape are being rapidly transformed.

> Global economic slowdown, climate change, global warming, growing uncertainty, stiff competition in the fight for market shares, the blurring of the thin line between business and corruption, and unrelenting proliferation in enterprises, products, and brands are putting tremendous pressure on businesses to survive, let alone grow, like never before.

Fast-paced advancements in technology, particularly in the digital area, whilst bringing about amazing paradigm shifts in the way we lead our lives, are also challenging people at the workplace to quickly acquire and adopt ever-changing skill sets. Fuelled by these developments, there is a kind of social, economic and political upheaval being experienced that impacts the psyche and well-being of all employees and entrepreneurs.

Employees are feeling increasingly 'burdened' at the workplace, thanks to heavy workloads, longer working hours and extremely demanding targets to achieve. As a result, their resilience and coping abilities are being rigorously tested. Insecurities also mount as workers fear the advent of pink slips and becoming victims of downsizing programs. Stressful conditions also lead to greater conflicts and it is not uncommon to find tensions at the workplace being 'carried' as accompanied baggage to homes and the family. Issues related to ethics being compromised by enterprises and non-alignment of individual value systems with those of the organisation only add fodder to the turbulence of employees caught in the mental tug-of-war raging within.

Owing to traditionally held beliefs that expected women to be the sole 'homemaker', working women were and still are expected to carry the load of domestic responsibilities and family obligations on their shoulders. Trying to achieve a work–life balance has thus been far more of a challenge and psychological strain for them compared to their male counterparts. In more recent times, however, some men, burdened by pressures of delivering on stiff performance objectives, are also feeling the strain of maintaining a work–life balance.

> Finding a career or entrepreneurial satisfaction in contemporary times within a very volatile and often chaotic environment has thus become one of the major determinants of our happiness quotient, and this is one of the key challenges we as a human workforce face.

Can a spiritual approach help cope with the challenges at the workplace? Is there a growing case for integrating the essence of spirituality into our work culture?

At first instance, spirituality at the workplace might sound like an abstract or metaphysical concept. But probe deeper and we might find there is a strong practical connect between our inner core self and the way we engage with our work life.

Spirituality at the workplace is not about inculcating religious dogmas or conditioning workers with any form of rituals to be followed. Nor is it about adhering to any belief system or 'ism' of any nature. It's about bringing to our work the true self rather than the programmed mind. It's about finding true purpose and meaning in our work, driven by our inner resolve, passion and spirit. It's about recognising that, at the very core of our being, there is a divine energy that one can tap into for wisdom. It is through the connection with this inner resource that we can actualise our dreams with truth, responsibility and integrity.

It's about the awareness that comes with the realisation that, whatever work we do is not just for our own personal purposes, but for a larger and more inclusive cause that we are also meant to serve wholeheartedly. This could mean taking responsibility for uplifting communities in society at large, or contributing to other selfless causes that touch people's lives in positive ways.

Let's deeply and honestly examine the relationship we have with our jobs or businesses.

> Would it not be true to say that if we feel unfulfilled in a particular role, it is usually on account of a host of factors that we perceive as missing on the **outside**—whether it is an insensitive, over-demanding and unrewarding boss, not enough freedom to operate, a paycheck that compares unfavourably with friends in other organisations, and so on?

In such situations it is normal for us to blame the organisation where we work, to crib and to feel disillusioned. This disenchantment then drives us to look around for alternative jobs that we feel will hold the promise of a truly satisfying career. However, more often than not, when we move on to the next role, we find that there is something or the other missing here too, and we wonder why we keep 'inviting' unfulfilling roles into our careers. Many might hold the view that it's no big deal in moving on to the next job. Sure, it's fine to feel that way, but only as long as we are certain that when we move on, the inherent 'problematic tendencies' also don't move on with us as well.

If we accept the guiding premise, as shared in earlier chapters, that fixing our life situations is not an outside job but an inner working that is required, that no one external to us is responsible for our emotional state, that nothing is intrinsically right or wrong, then we need to ask ourselves a few straight questions:

- Is there any such reality in our perception of being in a 'wrong' company, a 'wrong' role or with a 'wrong' boss at any point in time, because we have been programmed to play the blame game when situations are not to our liking? Does not the thought arise because we are driven by the ego whilst feeling isolated and disconnected from our true selves? Caught in the tentacles of the perceived problematic situation, do we not become unmindful of the fact that the universe is very much an involved co-partner in guiding our life's journey?

- What if we were to shift our perspective and view the situation differently, that whatever the organisation, role or boss we encountered at that moment in time was exactly what was meant for us, because we needed to learn some lessons from the experience? Maybe we have a habit of being over-critical, of not accepting responsibility, of procrastination, of being lazy, of not being fully committed to our work, and so on. Is it not possible, then, that our situation could be a mirror reflecting to us what aspects of ours need to transform before we begin to attract fulfilling experiences in our careers and businesses?

Let's face it—we have little or no control over the state of the economy, the work culture in any organisation, or the chaotic environment we operate in. We cannot expect bosses, colleagues or employees to change by conforming to our ways of working, or demand trust, respect and integrity from co-workers. These have to be earned. When we experience problems in interpersonal relations or get mired in conflicts, we usually end up playing the blame game, get angry, frustrated, lose our sense of mental equilibrium and start to curse the workplace. If we find no meaning or purpose in our work, we feel disgruntled and compromise our productivity and deliverables. It is the interplay of the 'troubled' mind that is actively at work, and consequently no solution can be conceived in such a state of turbulence.

It is in this context that spirituality may hold the answer for our work-related issues.

> Since spirituality is all about an inner connect and journey into an exploration of the self, it is this spiritual centre and richest resource we need to tap into for value-based answers that make our relationships with work and our career an enriching experience.

The following are some thought processes that could be mulled over and that support the case for integrating spirituality into overall work culture:

- Spirituality, in the context of work, is about unleashing your true passion through self-empowerment and infusing your spirit in what you do. When seen from a spiritual dimension, work is no longer just a set of tasks to be completed, like chores to be performed, and a paycheck to be received in return. It has a more profound meaning and serves a higher purpose. In such a situation, what you specifically do is of lesser consequence. What matters most is that whatever work you pursue is in total alignment with your heart's callings. You feel free, not having to submit to the expectations of others, who try to influence your choice of work. When you pursue what you love doing and enjoy it, you have no need to compare yourself to others; you motivate and stretch yourself to achieve maximum productivity for the organisation whilst experiencing a lot of inner satisfaction and contentment.

- Relating to work from a spiritual realm would mean we manifest virtues of humility, empathy, respect and compassion with all our co-workers. When these virtues come to the forefront, our ability to positively relate and respond to even the so-called 'difficult' people in the workplace is significantly enhanced. A rude, demeaning boss, then, need not be labeled as a 'terrible' boss to have. We may choose to see him in a different light—perhaps he is under tremendous pressure from his seniors and is merely reflecting this in his hostile interactions, has some unresolved personal issues that are finding an expression, and so on. By choosing not to react impulsively from the 'programmed' mind, but empathise with him, we may have possibly made a cause for the boss to examine the appropriateness of his outbursts, whilst not feeling unduly perturbed ourselves.
- A spiritual orientation motivates us to put in our very best. We no longer view our peers as 'competitors' or 'threats' and we see no need to play the game of the politics of one-upmanship or manipulation to run down our colleagues. Competing organisations are respected for what they are and since we operate from our true uncontaminated self, we do not feel the need to grow at their expense by resorting to unfair and unethical practices to run them down. Our prime focus is on raising the bar of our own performance through self-belief, unwavering commitment,

tenacity of purpose, and the vibrant energy we bring to enable the realisation of our goals.

- Conflicts, differences of opinions, and disagreements at the workplace are fairly common and may actually be a healthy sign because they reflect the existence of different perspectives and opinions, all which merit consideration before business decisions are taken. So the problem is not the presence of differences. The issue is how we respond to perspectives that may be different from ours. A spiritual bent of mind recognises and respects the need for everyone to express their viewpoint freely. It focuses on coming up with solutions in a fair, balanced manner without prejudices and insistence on holding preconceived notions that the ego relishes.

  The difference between a response coming from the conditioned mind and one coming from the inner self becomes clear when two questions, each representing differing mindsets, are considered:

> Who is right?
> (Coming from the ego.)
> *VS*
> What is right and best for the business?
> (Coming from the free spirit, which looks at the larger purpose, beneficial to the overall cause.)

The latter, collaborative mindset leads to a win-win situation for all, whilst the former vitiates the possibility of optimum solution-centric outcomes.

- It is now recognised that one of the most significant drivers for excellence at the workplace in times to come will be a relentless pursuit and application of innovation, creativity and lateral thinking.

> When you operate from the programmed mind, you give yourself little or no room and receptivity to allow fresh, new perspectives to present themselves to you.

However, when you connect with your true self, you are opening yourself to a whole world of possibilities because there is no limiting constraint or straitjacketed way of thinking your mind has imposed on itself. It is through this connection that new, revolutionary ideas are born and paradigm breakthroughs can be made. These serve to benefit humanity in a variety of ways.

- In modern times, the pursuit of mere financial goals by corporations through wealth maximisation of stakeholders is itself beginning to be questioned. Issues related to business ethics, global warming, environmental protection, human rights, equality between genders, shared responsibility for uplifting of communities, and other forms of corporate social responsibility programmes, are now beginning to receive attention by enterprises because they recognise the 'high cost' of disregarding and being indifferent to such issues.

  Truly speaking, at the core of such consideration is the premise that, operating from the ego dimension, humankind has only preoccupied itself with an endless stream of unfulfilled desires, chasing more and more of material wants whilst systematically ignoring the larger responsibility towards humanity.

Let's consider, as an example, the growing menace of environmental degradation and the degenerative impact of global warming that have grave implications not just for the sustainability of corporations but the very existence of planet Earth. It is no wonder, then, that this impending sense of crisis, looming large, brought more than 190 countries in Paris in 2015 to brainstorm on implementable solutions to safeguard planet Earth. If we were to probe deeper into the genesis of such problems through calm introspection, we might find that these issues, which have social, economic and political ramifications, are only *symptoms* of a much deeper malady.

If so, then can mere social-, political- or economic-centric solutions work?

Think about this: Are global warming and environmental deterioration not a consequence of some causes that have been made by the collective consciousness of human beings?

A little reflection would reveal that humans have systematically exploited and desecrated nature in various ways—whether by unabashedly cutting down trees, releasing toxic waste into rivers, depleting ozone levels, polluting the atmosphere with harmful and in some cases life-threatening particulate matter, or a host of other ways—all to pursue their selfish, vested interests.

> The question to ask ourselves is: In the final scheme of things, are all such developments not an outcome of the unrelenting **GREED** that the world today is consumed with?

Does it not indicate that the world wants to grow at an uncontrollably fast pace with no thought spared for the devastating consequences that are bound to follow through an abdication of responsibility towards a sustainable environment?

It might therefore be worth examining whether the events unfolding in the world are actually a mirror reflecting the states of human consciousness.

> Are these not actually manifestations of the core problem that one would like to term a '**spiritual deficit**'?

A spiritual perspective is therefore what would be required to bring about shifts in such mindsets, because spirituality recognises the interconnectedness of everything in this universe. Nothing exists in isolation, and the separateness we assume is fictitious, because it is only a projection of the mind. In the ultimate scheme of things, we are all part of the same universe and a manifestation of the same divinity. So, life or business is not about pursuing selfish, narrow interests but working responsibly and inclusively to bring about growth for the welfare of all we are connected to, and doing our individual bit to preserve nature, which gives in abundance for our own sustenance. The universe has enough to meet all of our *needs* but may never have enough to meet our unlimited *wants*. It is this transformation from a mindset of greed to one of contentment that holds the promise for our inner tranquility. As we continue on the evolutionary curve of our work and careers, we may find the pace of transformation of the business landscape increasing even more rapidly. Changes could be sweeping, with far-reaching consequences for humanity of a kind we may not have earlier experienced or even anticipated. Artificial intelligence, robots replacing labour in many industries, electric and even self-driving cars, cloning, explosion in data and information, are just a few examples of technological and structural changes that could impact the psyche of entire societies in a variety of ways. In his book, *Future Shock,* the eminent author Alvin Toffler alluded to a sense of disorientation and shattering stress people could increasingly experience as rapid transition was made to a 'super-industrial' society.

However, notwithstanding the pressures of unrelenting changes, when we are centred in our inner being with our connection with the free spirit, we can tap into our wellspring of courage, wisdom and determination to ride over all these changes with aplomb. We remain in awareness that whilst technology can be a great enabler, it does not have the power to consume us or determine our state of mind unless we allow it to do so. We realise that the life-changing situations we encounter have been created by the workings of the universe through the collective programming and consciousness of humanity. The choice, then, to respond to the changes no matter how traumatic they may appear, still rests with us.

What would it take to have satisfying and fulfilling work?

Having satisfying and fulfilling work doesn't come easy because there are a number of complex variables and factors interplaying with each other and impacting one's state of mind. Moreover, each person's perception of what makes for fulfilling jobs or businesses could be different, influenced by their own set of experiences and circumstances. Nevertheless, regardless of what you do, where you work, whether you are seeking your first job, looking for a change or contemplating being an entrepreneur, there must be some guiding considerations that hold promise of making your work satisfying and meaningful. Here they are for you to reflect on and assess whether they strike a chord of resonance:

- **Being guided by the inner voice that will direct you towards your heart's longings—to what you will love doing**

  What job/career/business/role/domain one should pursue is a fundamental and at times taxing decision many of us are confronted with at some stage of life or the other. Often a feeling arises of being at crossroads, confused by what choice we should exercise. The decision-making process becomes rather difficult because we are caught in the mental conditioning trap—expectations by family, advice by all and sundry, perceptions that get formed through inputs from media, pressures to adopt a bandwagon approach (because my friends think it's the 'in' thing to make a career in some particular industry domain and within that in a particular functional area), etc.

  When it's a question of major decisions that will deeply impact our lives ahead for many years, can our work choices be made on the basis of the conditioned mind—an aggregate of 'voices' that mostly belong to others but hardly to us?

> Deriving satisfaction from our work and having a fulfilling experience would require us to listen to only one voice, which is the true calling of our heart—a guiding beacon that just 'knows' where our mission would be best served. It would direct us to the kind of work we would truly love doing.

There is no reasoning, no logic, no rationalisation that has to be contended with. All we have to do is calmly listen to our inner voice by turning down the volume of all other interfering channels that are but a cluster of prejudices, biases, stereotypes and opinions of others. When you make your work choices on the basis of your 'inner voice', you bring forth a life force to your work in a manner such that you and you and your work are no longer separated but virtually one. Now, whether you choose to be a DJ, teacher, scientist, social worker, chef, writer, etc. ceases to matter to your true self. You just experience the joy of doing whatever you do because your heart and soul is totally in it.

> Fall in love with what you're going to do for a living. It's very important. To be able to get out of bed and do what you love for the rest of the day is beyond words. It's just great. It'll keep you around for a long time.
>
> —George Burns
>
> *American comedian, actor and writer*

- **Why let stress pin us down when the power to effectively cope and manage stress resides in the recesses of our inner being?**

  In contemporary times, humankind is becoming increasingly vulnerable to the syndrome of stress at the workplace. At first instance this would seem to be a natural fallout of heightened environmental pressures and increasing demands being placed on entrepreneurs and employees to deliver highly ambitious results. However, scratch the surface and you may find that whilst the environmental developments may be a trigger, they do not necessarily have to result in stressful conditions.

> This is because it is primarily our attitude that fuels stress. It is the making of a defeated mind that has convinced itself with a message: 'I am helpless to deal with the situation' or 'I do not have the emotional or physical strength to cope with pressures at work'.

Now, think about this: By adopting such an attitude, are we not draining ourselves of the vital energy required to handle our situation, no matter how daunting or challenging it may be? If our attitude is the cause of our stress, then it has to be a mental readjustment of attitude that can help us overcome it. It is here where taking recourse to a spiritual framework is necessary. Because our spiritual nature or the true self has no self-imposed limitations. It recognises that we are already self-empowered and can deal with any situation in our lives. All that is required is for us to believe that we have this reservoir of strength and to shift our programmed mind away from the defeatist platform that we have created. Then there is nothing to fear or worry about. Our inner wisdom guides us and we just need to apply ourselves with total diligence and commitment to our cause. Why not, then, direct all our energies constructively to do our best? Let the outcomes take care of themselves. The situation is no longer getting on top of us or tossing us around. We are now on top of our situation. So where is the stress anymore?

- **Aiming for success *vs* realising inner satisfaction**

  Success means different things to different people. Each person has their own perceptions and yardsticks for gauging their success. However, a number of pertinent questions arise in this context as follows:

  - Is success defined by one's own yardsticks or the yardsticks of society?
  - Is success a journey or a destination?
  - Is success only contingent upon the attainment of some tangible, measurable goals, or are there many 'soft' intangibles that also contribute towards the measure of success?
  - Is the phenomenal success story of a top movie star or the world's top-rated cricketer, for instance, any different from that of an Indian Army soldier, braving freezing temperatures of as much as minus 40 degrees Celsius, guarding the borders of his country, whilst its citizens sleep comfortably in their quilts?

Is it not a fact that success, as we understand it, is something measured by the benchmarks that society, or for that matter even the media, sets? So success is something that has been defined for us by the external world. Sure enough, meritorious accomplishments seen from the eyes of our external environment give our ego a massive boost. But what about the sense of inner satisfaction that we get from what we do, which has more permanence to it and does not depend upon anyone outside of us to experience it? Satisfaction, then, is measured by how our own heart feels, and ultimately isn't this what truly matters?

Inner satisfaction, in contrast to success, is about doing what you like and liking what you do with passion and joy, without any need to be evaluated by others. Nor does it necessarily have to be about attaining specific, measurable goals. It's more about how much we struggle to overcome the obstacles we encounter in life's journey; it's about the never-say-die spirit despite all misfortunes that came our way; it's about the unwavering commitment to relentlessly pursue our dreams without fear of failure.

> For when the One Great Scorer comes
> To mark against your name
> He writes not that you won or lost
> But how you played the Game.
>
> —Henry Grantland Rice
> *20th-century American sportswriter*

Satisfaction that emanates from the heart is determined not so much by the positions we attain in our careers or how much money we accumulate in our bank accounts. It stems from how much of our time and care we can give to make a positive difference to others. It's about what we did to wipe the tears and bring a smile to the faces of those who were in agony or were challenged—physically, emotionally or economically.

Satisfaction is about how selfless, responsible and caring we can be to our family, spending precious and treasured joyful moments with them, sharing with them our love and affection, rather than being caught in this ruthlessly materialistic world and mindlessly pursuing only narrow, self-serving interests.

It is also about how we use repeated failures as a springboard for our growth and for the realisation of our dreams.

- **There is no such thing as 'failure' in work**

Isn't it a fact that we grow up believing there are only negative connotations with 'failure'? After all, that is what we have been programmed to think. In the context of the workplace, we end up associating failure with not being able to get a job we wanted badly, our inability to achieve targets given to us, being denied a promotion that ultimately went to one of our colleagues, and so on. Whatever the reason, failure is something that has a deep, adverse impact on our psyche. It robs us of our self-confidence, creates self-doubt vis-à-vis our skill sets, increases our levels of insecurity, and weakens our self-image. The unfortunate outcome is that we make all these self-deprecating thoughts about ourselves the reality of our lives.

But let's just dispassionately think about the whole issue of failure. Is failure not just a mind construct? Is it not a self-imposed phenomenon? Is it not a mere reflection of a low self-belief and a denial of one's own inherent capabilities and potential? Societies world-over are largely conditioned to compartmentalise people as 'successes' or 'failures' depending on their own imaginations and interpretations. Why do we need to accept and internalise how the world views us?

What if we deconditioned ourselves and changed the filter with which we view failure? Can failure not be seen as a signal or a cue that points out what is not working for us and what internal changes or adaptations we need to make to get into an 'achievement' mode? Maybe we are out of tune with our inner callings and have gotten into a role that our heart wishes not to be in. Maybe we have not overcome some inherent tendencies of blaming only our environment and not taking personal responsibility, we are low in our determination and commitment, etc.

So we could always choose to perceive so-called failures as just mirrors reflecting back to us the changes required in our thinking, attitude and behavioural patterns. In doing so, failure is no longer self-defeating or 'negative', but just an instrument holding the seed for our transformational growth.

- **Why do we need to see ourselves as being in competition with others?**

In the fast-paced world that we live in today, do we not stress ourselves out because we feel we are caught in a rat race and need to constantly run ahead of others, driven by the fear of being left behind? Is it not these thoughts that result in our anxiety and cause mental turbulence? We feel insecure and dread competition—both from competing organisations and our own peers, whom we regard as possible barriers for us to move up the ladder. But let's ask ourselves: Is competition defined by our business environment? Or is it a meaning ascribed by our own minds and the way we perceive it? So consumed and intimidated do we get by self-professed notions of competition that our focus and even strategic thinking are centred around how we can dislodge and demolish competing companies whilst even running down our peers to get ahead. In doing so, at times we may also compromise ethics and our own value systems. We rationalise and justify our thinking with the belief that if we have to survive, let alone grow, we need to be ruthlessly competition-centric while devising our game plans.

But what are we trying to do—chase goals, aspirations and targets of competition? Do we not have our own visions and goals to pursue? Is our growth only possible through knocking down competition? Do we not have our own journey to undertake and relish? Is the race finally not ours only? Sure, from a tactical and strategic standpoint, it is important to be aware of what competition is doing, but surely we don't have to turn this into an obsession, disregard our own choices and deny ourselves our own goals.

So why lose sleep by constantly comparing our work, careers, or organisations to others'? What if we were to shift away from our programming and alter our mindset with a perspective that tells us: 'We are in competition with no one but our own selves'? Competition is no longer a 'monster' for us that needs to be decimated. It is what it is—another entity on its own corporate journey.

We no longer use competition as the benchmark to define our performance. Our performance gets defined by our own levels of attained excellence, the bar for which is continuously raised, and the dogged determination and unflagging zeal we bring forth to achieve nothing but the best for our own growth and the growth of our business or enterprise.

- **There is life beyond just work and paychecks with many perks**

We live in times where the compulsions of enterprises and businesses to remain competitive and keep themselves afloat puts incessant pressures on employees and entrepreneurs to devote more and more time to work. Thanks to technology and the proliferation of handheld devices such as iPads, mobiles, and even laptops, homes are becoming an extension of the workplace. The fear of missing out on hefty bonuses, inviting reprimand from superiors, being denied recognition, employees 'underperforming' on stiff deliverables, and entrepreneurs having to protect their businesses from going into the red, are just a few factors compelling us to overstretch ourselves on work schedules.

A study (survey 2015), instituted by the Apex Chamber of Commerce and Industry in India, Assocham, came up with some startling revelations.

As per the study, as much as a staggering 42.5 per cent of corporate employees in the private sector were found suffering from depression. Furthermore, mental problems, such as anxiety disorder and depression, had increased by 45–50 per cent among corporate employees in the last eight years. These illnesses and issues were being fuelled largely by demanding schedules, high stress levels and the pressure to attain performance-related perquisites.

Various other studies report the high incidence of health disorders such as frozen shoulders, stiff necks, carpet tunnel syndrome, lack of sleep, obesity, and hypertension, stemming largely from overwork and unduly long hours spent in front of computers, especially in professionals from metropolitan cities and those working in the IT sector. What is also significant is the increasing incidence of diminished libidos among couples and lack of any time for bonding or physical intimacy—so relentlessly occupied are they with observing late hours at offices or businesses or continuing their work at home. Clearly the boundaries between work life and family life are getting blurred. Isn't this a heavy price to pay for making work your sole raison d'être for your existence?

It could of course be argued that in many instances, people do not work long hours as a matter of choice. They do so because they have to struggle to make ends meet. Often they feel compelled to put in those long working hours in the belief that their employers may take unkindly to them and respond with some form of punitive steps. As such, expecting such people to look for life beyond just work may at first instance seem unreasonable. This aspect would find support in the theory of 'hierarchy of needs' that the eminent psychologist Abraham Maslow had propounded way back in the 40's. Despite some limitations, this theory is still accepted as a valid premise for understanding human motivation. According to this theory, people would require their basic physiological and security needs (elements required for survival including money) met before they feel motivated to pursue higher order needs of belongingness, self-esteem and self-actualisation (highest growth stemming from inner self-fulfillment). Untoward life experiences, however, such as illness, divorce, loss of job, etc.

could cause an individual to oscillate between different types of needs in the hierarchy. Maslow pointed out that only a small fraction of individuals become fully actualised .This is because society is conditioned to reward motivation largely based on monetary considerations, esteem, power and social standing.

Years after Maslow published his theory, he went on to submit a modification of his earlier submission. He observed that in quite some situations, people could graduate up the hierarchy without even the lower order needs being met. Specifically, he used the example of those economically challenged to assert that such individuals could motivate themselves through the quality of social networks and relationships. Should a strong supportive family and social ties be in place, it could be possible for individuals to compensate for the perceived 'insufficiency' of basic, first-order needs and strive for their advancement.

In a wide-ranging study of employee motivation conducted by Harvard Business School Professor Teresa Amabile and psychologist Steven Kramer, hundreds of employees were asked to highlight their single most important motivator. For 95 per cent of employees, it was not money, safety or security that was overwhelming. They believed that they brought out their best and achieved highest productivity when they got the feeling that they were making progress every day towards a meaningful goal.

It would therefore appear that, beyond a point, working for a paycheck by itself cannot be a sustainable motivating factor. People may work for money, but also take pride in working for a meaningful purpose and in a work environment that nurtures in the employees a sense of belonging.

If we carry out an honest, objective self-assessment, it may dawn upon us that we may be losing out on a lot in our lives by allowing ourselves to get sucked into the whirlpool of a chaotic rat race. For sure, it's good to have money and to be able to afford the comforts and luxuries of a good living. But the question is: At what cost? Is the unflinching pursuit of mere financial goals worth it if you are missing out on those very special moments of life—the smile on your children's face when you turned up at their skit performance despite being busy, the time you took off from work to take your spouse on a much-needed vacation to enjoy togetherness, or the ecstatic feeling you and your parents experienced when you decided to take time off and just be with them to savour the moment, etc.?

> Should we not be doing a self-introspection once in a while—whether, in the process of chasing more wealth and more acquisitions, we are not losing out on those soft intangibles which money can possibly never buy?

It's a fact—if you only run after jobs that offer you the best remuneration and perks, and work purely to amass larger wealth through your business, you are quite likely to be compromising your sense of inner satisfaction and fulfilment. Money, though important, has never been the defining benchmark for an enriching life, nor will it ever be. The defining benchmark is the quality of 'human connections' that you could nurture.

It is not surprising, therefore, to find the young generation today wanting more out of their lives than perhaps their parents did. According to a study conducted by Talentsmoothie, a firm of organisational development consultants, salary and status mattered less to Generation Y. What was high in their priority check-list were attributes such as doing work that they loved, flexible timings, opportunities for taking time out for travel and family, the choice to work from home, and an overall better work–life balance. It would thus appear that the modern generation seems determined not to make work the be-all and end-all of their lives. While they don't wish to shy away from work, they would rather choose to 'work to get the best out of life' rather than 'just live to work'.

Maslow's theory on 'need fulfilment' still has a lot of relevance in present times. Its framework provides challenges and opportunities for organisations to recognise that providing true meaning and purpose for all its employees (and not just the senior management) has to be viewed from a larger dimension, going beyond 'meaning from work' to 'meaning from life'.

> We are prone to judge success by the index of our salaries or the size of our automobiles rather than by the quality of our service and relationship to mankind.
>
> —Martin Luther King Jr
>
> *American civil rights activist*

- **Culturalising the workplace with values based on the essence of spirituality**

  If you are a leader in your respective business or enterprise, you may wish to consider culturalising the organisation with 'humanistic' values that would always work in the best interests of the company, its employees and the communities around. For this to happen, leaders have to take tremendous responsibility to personally demonstrate, at first instance, the highest standards of uncompromising ethics in their conduct and management of the workplace.

> Constant respect for each other's dignity, uncompromising ethics, remaining focused, inspiring the workforce to channelise their energies towards creativity and innovation, giving freedom to function, encouraging transparency, nurturing a climate of trust, being open to criticism, shedding arrogance, and reaching out to the cause of developing communities while walking the talk, are some of the core humanistic values that leaders or owners could adopt for making the workplace truly rewarding.

Why does the integration of these spiritual values into the mainstream culture of an organisation assume so much importance?

Firstly, because a great leader is one who never sacrifices the overall interests of the human resources at the altar of sheer monetary profits. Secondly, these values promote a climate for motivated employees who are more stable and far less stressed, resulting in higher productivity. Thirdly, it is increasingly becoming critical for enterprises to retain employees in whom they have invested a lot of time and money. When humanistic needs of the workforce are adequately met, they feel a strong sense of belonging with the organisation, strive to put in their very best and are not easily lured away by other organisations. Finally, when the leader and their team remain centred in their respective spiritual selves, there is a deep appreciation for empathy and compassion for one another. People no longer work with fear or insecurities but with joy. This is what makes for a truly satisfying and fulfilling work experience.

Contentment with your work is solely your outlook and your choice

Let's accept it—in the imperfect world that we are part of, there is not going to be any business set-up or enterprise that is tailor-made to our desired perception of an ideal workplace. We cannot always determine the work environment or culture where we work. However, what we can do is change our attitude and the manner in which we respond to the environment we have chosen to be part of.

When we operate from the spiritual realm (and that is a choice we can always make), we understand that contentment is going to come from within and not handed to us by the enterprise, or by our bosses or business leaders. Learning to reinvent ourselves, finding newer ways to make a difference, changing our perspective in terms of how we view our jobs, honing our skills, and having the willingness to keep learning and enhancing our domain knowledge, are just a few ways in which we can add value to our work. In choosing to do so we avoid falling into the routine, boring, drab pit, which many times we are prone to doing.

Exercising your preference to work with enterprises whose value systems are largely in sync with your own enables you to find a better 'fit' with the organisation and keeps you meaningfully and productively engaged.

If, however, you still find that there is a mismatch in values, and that despite your dedicated efforts to bring out your best you are not satisfied with the work environment, it may be time to do a reality check. If your heart sends out discomforting signals, you do not look forward to getting to work every day, you feel you are compromising a lot in terms of your work–life balance and inner peace of mind, it may be time to 'let go' and consider an alternative work environment, career, or role. Maybe you feel some stirrings inside of you calling you to start something of your own. At the end of the day it's your choice and you owe it to yourself not to remain trapped and disgruntled in a role that goes against your inner voice.

∞

7

THE ESSENCE OF A LIBERATING JOURNEY

"A liberating journey of life is not so much a state of mind as much as it is a state of 'no-mind'.

"It is in the letting go of all the false and limiting ideas, beliefs and stereotypes working against our growth that our emancipation lies. This, and the feeling that the universe is ever guiding us and carrying us along the path meant for us, can be truly liberating.

Even though the meaning of freedom may have differing connotations and interpretations amongst people, one thing can be agreed upon—all of us do seem to want it.

But many questions crop up when we talk about freedom since these would arise in different contexts.

- Is it about thinking, expressing and doing *whatever* we wish to, whenever we wish?
- Does it imply having the choices to create one's own sense of purpose and steering life in one's desired direction?
- Would freedom have to do with seeking liberation from the shackles of external forces, be it religious dogmas, societal norms or various environmental obstacles and strictures?
- Or on the other hand, is freedom something dependent only on an 'inner' working in the sense of overcoming self-created barriers and tendencies that limit us? When we are no longer prisoners of our conditioned minds and start living in accordance with our free spirit?
- Can freedom to act in any situation be exercised without a sense of responsibility also accompanying it?
- Is freedom something that one seeks as an end in itself? Would it even be relevant if it were not to be harnessed for a creative purpose to realise one's self-actualisation goals?

And the list could go on.

Whenever we talk in terms of freedom, it is a natural supposition that we are seeking some kind of liberation and this is invariably from something outside of us. However, let's ask ourselves—even though we may have got our independence from foreign rule or are enjoying all our rights and privileges granted to us by the State, have our freedom of speech, etc.—*are we really free in the true sense of the word*?

Think about this: Can we be truly free and independent if:

- We still remain prisoners of our own past, chained to our conditioned minds in which lie dumped all sorts of beliefs, ideas and opinions not only of others but of ourselves, which rule our thoughts, feelings and behaviours?
- We carry the immense burden of all our worries, anxieties, fears, bitterness, regrets, grudges, expectations, self-limiting barriers, and need to conform to the will of others, all of which bind us and prevent us from truly creating and experiencing a life that is a reflection of our inner truth.
- We continue to hold everyone else, the outside circumstances and situations, responsible for our problematic life and misery, thereby wallowing in self-pity.

> Some people live in cages with bars built from their own fears and doubts. Some people live in cages with bars built from other people's fears and doubts; their parents, their friends, their brothers and sisters, their families. Some people live in cages with bars built from the choices others made for them, the circumstances other people imposed upon them. And some people break free.
>
> —C. Joybell. C
> *Eminent thinker and writer*

What then would be the essence of a truly liberating journey of life?

If it is our identification with thoughts in the mind that keeps us entrapped and entangled, it would follow that any liberating journey of life must start with a de-identification with the mind. The subconscious mind, which is nothing but a repository of programmed thoughts, beliefs and behaviour patterns, would continue to use us and direct our lives, if we believed 'we are the mind'.

> The mind can be a great instrument and tool, but only if we use it productively for creating value. It is otherwise a terribly destructive piece when we allow it to ensnare us, master us and use us. We end up being slaves of our mind. Our very existence becomes caged. So where then is the question of experiencing our true freedom?

So if the stored impressions in the mind are self-defeating and limiting, which they often are, we find it difficult to nurture a positive outlook towards life. This is because we remain in the vice-like grip of a mind that merely reflects our negative thoughts and attitude.

> If you're determined to think of yourself as limited, fearful, vulnerable, or scarred by past experience, know only that you have chosen to do so. The opportunity to experience yourself differently is always available.
>
> —Yongey Mingyur Rinpoche
> *Tibetan Buddhist meditation master*

However, once we drop our identification with the mind, the mind becomes a separate entity from our true self. We can now 'master the mind' and use it creatively and constructively. In doing so, we begin to feel truly 'free'.

Real freedom to do something can make sense only when we act out of awareness and make conscious choices, being in the moment—the now. It cannot also be about doing anything we want to, because invariably our actions are performed with the conditioned mind driving us through its preset programmes. As such the free will cannot come into operation.

Nor can true freedom be devoid of responsibility. We can't say we will cherish our freedom to act in a manner of our choosing but shirk the responsibility of our actions. So freedom and responsibility must be concomitant.

> True freedom is always spiritual. It has something to do with your innermost being, which cannot be chained, handcuffed, or put into a jail.
>
> —Osho
>
> *Indian mystic and spiritual teacher*

A liberating journey thus would require us to lead a life of authenticity wherein we are being what we really are and not the false image that the mind projects to the outside world. Wherein choices are made on the basis of what we feel deep within to be true. And only that which comes from the heart or the free spirit can be true, not which comes from the working of the ego, which is all illusory. The freedom we enjoy now comes from being unaffected by what other people think of us and choosing not to let them determine our moods, emotions and behaviour.

> The most important kind of freedom is to be what you really are. You trade in your reality for a role... You give up your ability to feel, and in exchange, put on a mask. There can't be any large-scale revolution until there's a personal revolution, on an individual level. It's got to happen inside first.
>
> —Jim Morrison
> *American musician*

We begin to feel more free when we start to disregard thoughts of 'what could have been', or 'what should be' and replace these with 'what is', and just be in alignment with the moment. In doing so we drop all our inner resistance and just let things be as they are. We choose to go with the flow, the current of which is powered by a higher intelligence—by existence itself. If so, there is no fear in letting go, no concerns for safety or security, because our inner self, which is connected to existence, knows that we will never be carried on a path that does not work in our best interests. The liberating experience comes with the wisdom that life does not always have to have a destination. If the journey is fulfilling, why should a destination matter? We do not struggle with ourselves to go on chasing wants because, seen from a different perspective, life is not about becoming something or the other. That is a need only of the ego.

> Sometimes not being in control, not being able to think, just losing yourself in the moment, is the greatest feeling in the world. It's liberating. It's addicting. It's the most powerful high you'll ever get. It's a kind of freedom that tastes so sweet on your palate that you can't help but want more each time you have it.
>
> —Mia Asher
> *Writer*

Does that mean we merely sit back, take no action and wait for life to unfold for us? No. We do perform our tasks, but actions taken are inspired by the divine intelligence residing in our hearts rather than by the impulses of our programmed and manipulated minds.

In following the callings of our heart we can apply ourselves wholly to whatever stimulates us (whether it is work, painting, dancing, playing a musical instrument or a sport, just being with nature, etc.), without any judgements and any attachment to outcomes. Being fully alive in that activity, we may find that, while the mind may not get *totally* silenced, the chances of thoughts disturbing us and creating inner turmoil become much fewer. When we keep reprogramming ourselves to listen less to the chatter of the mind and more to the inner voice of wisdom that guides us in our daily choices, we facilitate our liberating journey. Giving more attention to this inner voice helps us let go of all the junk accumulated in the mind that has been working as a roadblock to our freedom, growth and contentment.

> From a practical standpoint, this could mean mustering the courage to discontinue being in a relationship, job, situation or circumstance that is creating an inner dissonance and requires us to operate against the grain of our true self.

Does having a liberating journey mean that the sailing will always be smooth? That we won't come across challenging situations that will try to pull us down? No. Every situation in life is subject to constant change. So if there are times of joy there will also be times of sorrow. But when we consciously choose to operate from the true self, we no longer have to feel helpless or hopeless, because the inner wisdom we have access to will show us the way to fearlessly tackle our situation, no matter how difficult it may be. And this is a great liberating feeling.

There is a momentary gap between all the stimuli in life triggered by events we encounter and our response to these stimuli. It is in this gap that the choice in terms of how we respond to whatever comes our way can be made. It is through this choice that the nature of our life's journey will get determined. This is what gives us our sense of tranquility and freedom.

Every moment of our life places a choice before us. No matter what our situation, circumstances or feelings, we can either act out of attachment to the false ego or out of our inner free spirit—an embodiment of truth and love. So now it's up to us to make the choice. Perhaps the following words of wisdom might find a resonance of affirmation:

> I Choose…
> to live by choice, not by chance;
> to make changes, not excuses;
> to be motivated, not manipulated;
> to be useful, not used;
> to excel, not to compete.
> I choose self-esteem, not self-pity.
> I choose to listen to my inner voice,
> Not the random opinion of others
> I choose to be me.
>
> —Miranda Marrott
> *Essayist*

Perhaps the greatest liberating experience would be in the awareness that, as we evolve in our journey of life, we are steadily and surely freeing ourselves from the self-defeating prisons that the programmed mind had constructed and kept us in.

∞

Acknowledgements

There are many people who have helped make this book a reality. I would like to acknowledge and express my deepest gratitude to them.

Firstly, my salutations to the divine energy of the universe that prompted me through my heart to write this book and guided me in this journey.

My heartful thanks to:

My family. To start with, my mother, Uma. You are not just an adorable soul but an endearing friend, full of love and compassion. Discussing the contents of the book with you and listening to your innate wisdom was very uplifting. I feel blessed to have you in my life, mom.

My sister, Deepa, and brother-in-law, Amrit. You both have hearts of gold and have always been there to support and encourage me in all my endeavours and pursuits.

My niece, Devika, and nephew, Pankaj. Your childlike innocence, affectionate nature and curiosity to know in detail about what I was planning to write has been touching.

Hema Rao, for the long stimulating sessions we had discussing the essence of what I planned to write, and for the crisp inputs and words of wisdom you readily shared.

All at Niyogi Books—the publishers of this book. In particular, I am grateful to:

Bikash, Tultul, and Trisha Niyogi, for believing in me and for your constant support.

Nirmal Kanti Bhattacharjee, for your valuable guidance.

Saachi Khurana, for your incisive observations and suggestions, patience and doing a great job editing this book. It has been a pleasure working with you.

Nabanita Das, for designing the book cover.

The entire production team at Niyogi Books.

Thanks also to many of my dear friends and relatives, who showed keen interest in the subject matter of this book. You all have been a great source of moral support and encouragement.

Finally, I am indebted to all the people who came into my life. You were the mirrors reflecting back what I most needed to learn about myself. It is this learning that has helped me evolve and grow as an individual.

Ajay Sachdeva graduated in Mathematics from St. Xavier's College, Mumbai. This was followed by a postgraduate degree in Operations Research from Delhi University. For securing first rank in this course at the university, he is the recipient of a gold medal. He went on to pursue a two-year Management programme from IIM, Ahmedabad. This is his first book.

He has over 37 years of rich experience working with several leading Indian and multinational corporations. His key areas of expertise include marketing, business strategy, and managing start-up ventures.

Recently, he retired as the managing director of an Indo–British joint venture enterprise, which he helped build from scratch. Ajay now mentors a few start-up ventures and is also a visiting faculty member at Bharatiya Vidya Bhavan, New Delhi.

His interests include reading, travelling, music, badminton and chess. Of late, he has taken to writing on spirituality. Many of his articles have been published in the *Awakening Times*, an e-magazine published in Serbia, and also in the blogs of the *Speaking Tree*.

Ajay currently lives in New Delhi and can be reached at asachdeva655@gmail.com